D1060545

STUDIES IN MODERN EUROPEAN
LITERATURE AND THOUGHT

General Editor:

ERICH HELLER

*Professor of German
in the University College of Swansea*

LERMONTOV

LERMONTOV

BY

JANKO LAVRIN

BOWES & BOWES
LONDON

PG
3337
L 4
L 41x

*Printed in Great Britain
by Richard Clay and Company Ltd,
Bungay, Suffolk*

CONTENTS

I. The Biographical Background . 9

II. A Poet's Progress . . . 32

III. Lermontov and the Romantic Mind 47

IV. The Climax 62

V. The Hero and the Age . . 76

VI. The Last Phase . . . 92

VII. Conclusion 106

Biographical Note . . . 108

Bibliography 109

The translations of Lermontov's verse reprinted in this study, *Borodino* and *My Country* (Frances Cornford and Esther Polyanóvsky Salaman) and *Gratitude, O Gloomy and Dreary* (C. M. Bowra), as well as *Testament* (Maurice Baring) and *When o'er the Yellowing Corn* (Walter Morison), originally appeared respectively in *Poems from the Russian* (Faber) and *A Book of Russian Verse* (Macmillan).

The translations of *A Hero of Our Time* by Eden and Cedar Paul are reprinted by permission of Messrs. George Allen & Unwin Ltd.

I

The Biographical Background

Lérmontov still continues to puzzle both historians of literature and his readers. The more one learns about him the more complex does he appear as a personality and as a poet. In contrast to Pushkin's genius, which was all of a piece, the genius of Lermontov cannot but strike one by those antinomies which were so typical of Lermontov the man. It is all the more surprising that in spite of his early death at the age of twenty-six, he yet left a literary heritage the best of which is of the highest order. And however 'Russian' he may have been in his work and feelings, he is of special interest to British readers on account of his distant Scottish origin, going back to the Lermonts or Learmonths of Ercildoune.

One of his ancestors was, presumably, the thirteenth-century bard Thomas the Rhymer, who, according to popular tradition, had spent seven years among the fairies. Sir Walter Scott's *Contribution to Minstrelsy of the Scottish Border* actually opens with three folk ballads about the Rhymer who had been enticed into the Elfland by the Fairy Queen herself.

> 'Harp and carp, Thomas,' she said,
> 'Harp and carp along with me,
> And if you dare to kiss my lips,
> Sure of your body I will be.'

As he was more than willing to kiss her lips, he became her sweetheart and stayed with her full seven years. After that he was released, but only on condition that at a given sign he would return without fail. One day, when Thomas was carousing with his friends in the castle of Ercildoune, a hart and a hind came from the near-by forest and with stately dignity passed by. Taking leave of his companions, Thomas followed the two animals into the forest, and was never seen or heard of again. So much for the earliest known Lermont.

Another less legendary but more real Lermont appeared some four centuries later, in Poland of all places. In the wars between Poland and Russia during the 'troubled period' (at the beginning of the seventeenth century), the Polish army included a contingent of Scottish and Irish soldiers. In 1613 the Poles were rather hard pressed in the region of Smolénsk. So about sixty of these mercenaries thought that it might be more 'expedient' to join the Russians and fight the Poles instead. This they did. Among the deserters was the poet's ancestor George Lermont, whose defection soon brought him the rank of an officer and (in 1621) several villages in the province of Kostromá. The Scottish Lermont thus became the Russian Lermontov. But a certain nostalgia for Scottish hills and heather must have lingered on in the family. Anyway, the poet Michael Lermontov refers in two of his youthful poems to Scotland as his mother country. He also seems to have inherited certain Scottish features as ingredients of his own character. Nonconformity, independence, a kind of dour pride and reserve were among them. Combined with Slav emotionality and moodiness, such features were bound to lead, especially in the Russia of those days, to all sorts of complications.

A further point to be stressed is the impact of English romanticism (notably of Byron) upon Lermontov. Byron's influence on Pushkin, for instance, was transient. It only helped him to find the essence of his own genius which was different from that of the English poet. The affinities between Byron and Lermontov went however much deeper: they were spiritual and temperamental, due to a similar attitude towards life and the world; so much so that his discovery of Byron's works determined as it were the main trend of Lermontov's own poetic development. Here we have a case of parallelism, rather than a passive following or imitation. This only makes an excursion into his life and activities all the more worth while, especially if we approach them against the background of the Russia in which he lived.

Mikhaíl (Michael) Yúryevich Lermontov was born in Moscow on 15 October (new style) 1814, the son of Yúry Lermontov—an impoverished landowner and captain in retirement who had married far above his social status. His wife was the only daughter of the widowed Elizavéta Arséneva [1]: a member of the wealthy Stolýpin family. Owning the large property of Tarkhány (in the Pénza province) and also a house in Moscow, the overbearing Mme Arséneva was strongly attached to her nervous and ailing daughter, but never bothered to conceal her contempt for her insignificant son-in-law. When her grandson Michael was only six months old, she took him to her distant country village and made his father a nominal manager of her estate, but the two never got on well together. Nor was there much love lost between Lermontov senior and his wife, who died of consumption some four years after her marriage. Michael's father then left Tarkhány, and his son remained in the sole care of Mme Arséneva, who lavished on him all her affection and actually made of him a fetish.

Having lost his mother at the age of three, the future poet was bound to experience, even as a child, that feeling of loneliness which remained with him throughout his brief life. At the same time the way he was pampered and idolized

[1] Her husband committed suicide in 1811.

tended to make him regard his own ego as the centre of the world. On the other hand, his pedantic German nurse bullied him so much with her rules of propriety as to make him hate from an early age any enforced authority. His rebellious disposition was moreover fostered by the things he saw on the estate of his autocratic grandmother, who treated her serfs as chattels.

One great advantage he enjoyed was a good private education. Mme Arséneva engaged Russian and foreign tutors from whom the boy could acquire a passable general knowledge and more than a passable mastery of French and German. Among his unforgettable experiences were, however, the three journeys to the Caucasus he had made in the company of his grandmother before he was twelve. On each of these occasions he stayed near the fashionable spa of Pyatigórsk with the Elborous group of mountains looming in the distance. The gorgeous panorama made such an impression on the boy that henceforth the Caucasus became the land of his 'heart's desire', destined to play a conspicuous part in his literary work, his adult life and—finally—in his tragic death.

In the autumn 1827, in his fourteenth year, Lermontov went with his grandmother to Moscow, where he was admitted to the privileged 'Pension noble' attached to Moscow University. Counting among its one-time pupils the two dramatists Fonvízin and Griboyédov, the poet Zhukóvsky, and the philosopher Chaadáyev, the school prided itself on its literary tradition. Also its educational methods were of an advanced and liberal kind.[1]

Writing as well as the translating of poetry was in the school's curriculum, and Lermontov excelled in both. Nor did he neglect adequate reading. In addition to the best Russian poets of the day (Zhukóvsky, Bátyushkov and, above all, Púshkin) he read French and German authors. He also acquired a sufficient knowledge of English to enjoy Byron's works in the original.

After two years profitably spent in the 'Pension noble' Lermontov entered (in 1830) the University of Moscow. That was at a time when his poetic urge, immature though it was, reached its first peak as far as sheer quantity of output was concerned. He had also shown considerable talent as a musician and especially as a painter. It was in Moscow, too, that he had his first love affairs. In the house of his relatives, the Stolý-pins, he was able to meet a number of young girls, mostly cousins or second cousins, with whom he kept falling in love—one after the other—only to be awakened to the fact that he was not a ladies' man. The reason was probably his unprepossessing appearance, the awareness of which must have been responsible for quite a few complexes in his character.

Lermontov's period of puberty set in at an

[1] This was the reason why in 1830 Nicholas I ordered the school to be closed and then turned into an ordinary Grammar School.

early age. His need of love, 'romantic' and otherwise, was unusually intense. But so were his disappointments. When hardly sixteen, he fell in love with Nadya Ivánova (the daughter of a Moscow dramatist) and then with the pretty but flighty Ekaterína Sushkóva, neither of whom took him seriously. Lermontov swallowed his hurt pride; and touchy as he was he never forgave nor forgot. In the case of Sushkóva he even took a mean revenge years later, when he met her in St. Petersburg. A much more serious case was his infatuation for Várya Lopúkhina—perhaps the only true love in his life. Yet even Várya betrayed him when, in May 1835, she suddenly married the wealthy and mediocre N. F. Bakhmétyev—a man twice her age. Lermontov was thus compelled to develop at an early age a cold and flippantly ironical attitude towards women simply as a safeguard against similar experiences. In spite of this, he never got over his love for Várya.

Another complication which arose in Moscow was due to the presence of Lermontov's father. The exact attitude of Lermontov to his parent is still difficult to assess. All we know is that in Moscow his father often came to see him and even insisted on having a say in the boy's education. The quarrels which ensued on this account between him and Mme Arséneva were hardly of an edifying nature. Perhaps it was to the good of all concerned that Lermontov senior died suddenly in 1831. The poem his son wrote on that occasion shows affectionate pity rather than the kind of love which comes from respect.

In the meantime, Lermontov attended lectures at the University. He remained there two years only. But those two years coincided with the period when that institution was beginning to play a leading part in Russian culture as a whole.

3

In order to understand the importance of Moscow University for the cultural life of Russia during the 1830's one must first mention some consequences of the revolt raised on 14 December (O.S.) 1825 against Nicholas I. The revolt itself, led by the liberal-minded nobles, known since then as the 'Decembrists', was a delayed explosion of the discontent going back to the hopes aroused by the victorious campaign against Napoleon in 1812. One should not forget that the actual leadership of Russian literature, thought and culture in general, was in those days almost entirely in the hands of educated members of the nobility and gentry, who pinned their expectations on the supposed liberalism of Alexander I. But it was all to no purpose. Once Napoleon had been beaten the victorious Tsar plunged into a kind of pseudo-mysticism, leaving the affairs of the world to the sadistic reactionary Arakchéyev and his kind.

Such a political climate, far from appeasing the dissatisfied elements, only drove their discontent underground. The young nobles who not so long ago had fought the invader now found the only outlet for their cheated hopes in secret societies. Two of these—the Southern and Northern Unions—had quite a strong membership in St. Petersburg as well as in the Ukraine. The difficulties arising after the sudden death of Alexander I were seized upon by discontented officers in the Guards as the right moment for a revolt. It all started as a protest against the notorious martinet Nicholas I, who had ascended the throne instead of his brother Constantine. Unfortunately, the revolt itself was badly organized. Nor did it find any support or understanding among the masses. The soldiers who came out, with their officers, to fight in the Senate Square for a more liberal Russia, had been given the slogan 'Constantine and Constitution'. But many of them thought that Constitution (Konstitútsiya in Russian) was Constantine's wife. No wonder the revolt was quelled in no time. What followed was the usual aftermath of horror. Five of the ringleaders, including the poet Ryléyev, were hanged. Another 120 'Decembrists', belonging to the best families in Russia, were sent to the Siberian mines—for most of them a kind of execution by instalments. At home again the severest police-regime was imposed—with Prussian thoroughness—by such a time-server of German extraction as Count Benkendorf.

Despite its failure, the 'Decembrist' revolt became a landmark not only in the political but also in the cultural life of Russia. For one thing, it put an end to the gentry-period of Russian culture and paved the way for the 'intelligentsia'—that peculiar amalgam of gentry intellectuals and educated commoners who gradually took over the leadership in these matters and remained the actual guardians of Russian culture roughly from the 1840's until the Revolution of 1917.

In the civil service, too, the members of the nobility suffered a decline. As the government no longer trusted them implicitly, it opened wide the gate to professional careerists of all classes, provided they were willing to serve without harbouring any 'dangerous thoughts'. Besides, these were quickly stamped out by Benkendorf's ubiquitous gendarmes, who did not shrink even from inspecting the private correspondence of the Tsar's subjects. Such and similar measures were further reinforced by Count Uvárov's official trinity of 'Autocracy, Orthodoxy and Nationalism', proclaimed in 1833 as the pivot for all law-abiding citizens.

Still, the liberal spirit of opposition as bequeathed by the 'Decembrists', was not crushed. It was particularly strong among the younger intellectuals who studied at Moscow University at the beginning of the 1830's—a decade when the University of Moscow became the actual focus of Russian culture, as well as the nursery of subsequent leaders in Russian thought and literature.

An important factor of the University life were

the debating circles organized by the students. The circle presided over by Stankévich was particularly active. German philosophy of the day—the philosophy of Schelling and that of Hegel—formed the centre of their interests. Herzen, on the other hand, gathered around him youngsters who were interested in social problems. Humanitarian and utopian–socialist theories, coming from France, became a further stimulating influence, at least within the University walls.

4

It is significant, though, that during his two years of University studies Lermontov (like Goncharóv) refrained from taking part in any circles and activities where he would have to mix with other students. He preferred to be left alone. Whether this was due to the shyness of a self-absorbed youth, to snobbery, or to both, is difficult to say. Yet his mind and talent were feverishly active all the time. Those were in fact the first years of his literary apprenticeship. Without intending to print anything as yet, he wrote between 1828 and 1832 some three hundred poems, seventeen Byronic tales in verse, and three plays.

It is true that in these early works his imagination ran ahead of his life-experience. It is equally true that he often emulated Byron to the extent of deliberately exaggerating his own gloomy *mal du siècle* and estrangement from ordinary mortals. In spite of this one cannot help feeling even in his juvenile verses considerable mental and emotional precocity. Nor can it be denied that his basic attitude towards life—that of protest—sounded genuine enough to be his own rather than borrowed from Byron. And his hatred of tyranny, the hatred he shared with all progressive minds of his generation, bore the stamp of the 'Decembrist' spirit, which was not foreign to his grandmother's family: her brother had been on friendly terms with the executed civic poet Ryléyev.

In 1832 Lermontov, for somewhat obscure reasons, left his Moscow alma mater and went to St. Petersburg. But as Petersburg University refused to take into account his two years of studies in Moscow, he gave up the University altogether and entered the School of Cavalry Cadets instead. Here he had to endure two years of the tedious soul-destroying barracks atmosphere, but on the surface at least he adapted himself to it well enough. Supplied with ample means by his grandmother, he took part in all sorts of drunken bouts, and even wrote unprintable bawdy verses suitable only for such occasions. The same style of life was continued by him after his promotion to ensign in the Hussar regiment stationed at Tsárskoe Seló—within easy reach of St. Petersburg.

The curious point, however, was that during all that time neither his loose living nor his writing of pornographic verse could silence his romantic love for Várya (or Várenka) Lopúkhina. This was only one of the numerous instances of his divided personality, of which he was fully aware and from which he often suffered morally. His moral *Katzenjammer* is evident in this passage taken from the letter he wrote in French to Várya's elder sister Maria on 23 December 1834:

'It is you alone I dare be sincere with, it is you alone who know how to be sorry for me without humiliating me, since I keep humiliating myself; and because there was a time when you calmed my acutest grief, you will perhaps chase away with your sweet words this cold irony which creeps into my soul irresistibly like water into a cracked boat.' [1]

And is it not strange that the same Lermontov should have complained about a year after, in a letter he sent from Tarkhány to his friend S. A. Rayévsky (16 January 1830), of being unable to have the usual sexual relations with serf-girls 'because they stink'?

Another complication arose out of Lermontov's position in a class-ridden society. In spite

[1] Ce n'est qu'avec vous que j'ose être sincère, ce n'est que vous qui savez me plaindre sans m'humilier, puisque je m'humilie déjà moi-même; et peut-être puisque autrefois vous avez calmé un chagrin bien vif, peut-être voudrez-vous maintenant chasser par de douces paroles cette froide ironie qui se glisse dans mon âme irrésistiblement comme l'eau qui entre dans un bateau brisé.

of his grandmother's wealth and connections, he was yet aware of the fact that his own father's place had been on the lower rungs of the gentry. Even as an ensign in the Guards he was often tolerated rather than accepted as an equal by his aristocratic fellow-officers. And however much he wished to become an habitué of the higher circles in the Russian capital, he knew they were inaccessible to him—a thing which hardly gratified his pride. Count V. A. Sollogúb says in his *Vospominánya* (*Reminiscences*): 'Lermontov, who was my friend of long standing, came of a good gentry family, but did not belong to the inner core of Petersburg society. Yet he was fond of it; he raved about it, even when ridiculing it as we sinners did.'

During the years of his military training (and immediately after) Lermontov's poetic output became much smaller than before. He kept experimenting also with plays and with prose—partly because he still felt uncertain of his talent. He achieved, however, his first triumph early in 1837 with a poem which made his name familiar among intellectuals all over Russia. On 29 January Pushkin died after his fatal duel with d'Anthès. It was on that occasion that Lermontov poured his gall and indignation into his *Smert poéta* (*The Death of a Poet*). Such a poem of indictment could not appear in print,[1] yet it

---

[1] It was first printed in 1856 in the Russian periodical *Polyárnaya Zvezdá* (*The Polar Star*), edited and printed in London by A. Herzen.

spread in thousands of written copies and was particularly relished after Lermontov had added another sixteen lines attacking the court circles who were guilty of Pushkin's untimely death.

Lermontov's sudden fame, slender though it was, had to be paid for. No sooner had the authorities found out that he was the author of that scathing poem than he was put under arrest and sent to an infantry regiment stationed in the wilds of the Caucasus. Those were the days when Russian troops were periodically called upon to pacify the Caucasian mountaineers with whom revolt seemed to be endemic. Lermontov was glad to see again the regions he had admired as a boy. He now spent several months in a remote fortress where he had ample leisure to collect his thoughts and creative energies. Far from missing his Petersburg companions, he wrote to Rayévsky: 'At the moment I have no wishes. I would gladly remain in this place and watch its scenery to the end of my days.'

The Caucasus gave him incentive for further creative efforts. This time he wrote no longer as an experimenter, but as a mature poet who had fully mastered his craft. It was here that he found at last a background suitable not only for his two best tales in verse *Mtsýri* (*The Novice*) [1] and *Démon* (*The Demon*), but also for his excellent novel *Geróy náshego vrémeni* (*A Hero of our Time*). Meanwhile the enterprising Mme

[1] Lermontov gave it this Georgian (and not Russian) title.

Arséneva had mobilized all her relatives and acquaintances (Count Benkendorf included) to get her grandson back to St. Petersburg. As a result the poet obtained the Tsar's permission to leave the Caucasus in the autumn of the same year. On his return he served for a while in the Gródno regiment stationed at Nóvgorod, but in January 1838 he was allowed to rejoin his old Hussar regiment of the Guards. This brought him back to Tsárskoe Seló and St. Petersburg.

5

This time Lermontov's return to the capital was something of a triumph. Having had several poems printed in periodicals during the months of his exile, he was now looked upon as the new hope of the Russian Parnassus, indeed as a successor to Pushkin. Even the 'cream of society' condescended to taking notice of him. He was lionized by the great ladies to whom only a year before he would have meant nothing. But whether sincerely or from inverted snobbery, Lermontov now pretended to be bored by it all, however gratified he may have felt in secret. There is a great deal of naive boasting in the letter he wrote (in French) to Maria Lopúkhina at the end of 1838 or the beginning of 1839:

'I must tell you, that I am the unhappiest of mortals, and you will believe me when you learn that every day I go to some ball or other, I am launched in high society: for a whole month I have been in fashion, they have been fighting for my company. All these people, whom I offended in my verses, are now glad to surround me with flatteries, the prettiest women beg verses from me and boast of them as of a triumph. All the same I feel bored. I demanded that I should be sent to the Caucasus: refused.' [1]

In the same letter he yet admits with obvious relish: 'Agree that one can get intoxicated by all this.' [2]

His intoxication did not last long. As if prompted by his own snobbery in reverse, Lermontov began to assert himself against his social betters by a deliberate and often arrogant lack of manners. In consequence he was soon treated as an undesirable outsider. Even his friend, Count Sollogúb, eventually ridiculed him —in his story *Bolshóy Svet* (*High Society*)—as a social climber. Nor did the poet cultivate the

[1] Il faut vous dire que je suis le plus malheureux des hommes et vous me croirez quand vous saurez que je suis chaque jour au bal; je suis lancé dans le grand monde: pendant un mois j'ai été à la mode, on se m'arrachait. Tout ce monde que j'ai injurié dans mes vers se plait à m'entourer de flatteries, les plus jolies femme me demandent des vers et s'en ventent comme d'un triomphe. Néanmoins, je m'ennuie. J'ai demandé d'aller au Caucase: refusé!

[2] Convenez que tout cela peut enivrer.

company of professional men of letters. He was acquainted though with Zhukóvsky. Later he saw now and then Belínsky who, in 1839, became the principal critic in *Otéchestvennye Zapíski* (*The Fatherland's Annals*)—a progressive monthly, founded in 1839, to which Lermontov contributed regularly.

It should be noted that in Tsarist Russia voluminous monthly periodicals played a more important part than anywhere else in Europe. For one thing, the daily press, muzzled as it was by the censors, could not discuss freely any problems of the day, let alone broader issues. A certain amount of independent views were smuggled in, however, in the guise of *belles lettres*, or else camouflaged by a kind of 'Aesop language' subtle enough to elude the vigilance of the censors—a practice fraught with risks for both writers and editors.

Yet strangely enough, those years of organized obscurantism and political witch-hunting marked the rise of Russian literature on the one hand, and the gradual birth of the intelligentsia on the other. After Pushkin's death Lermontov was in the ascendant, while such poets as Zhukóvsky, Baratýnsky and Tyútchev continued their work at a high level. In prose Gogol was going from one triumph to the other. In criticism the authority of Belínsky asserted itself sufficiently to stimulate, during the next decade, a galaxy of talents, such as Dostoévsky, Turgénev, Goncharóv, Písemsky and the dramatist Ostróvsky.

As for Lermontov, he reached the peak of his creative power in the second half of the 1830's, roughly between 1836 and 1841. And it was Belínsky who became his principal champion and admirer. He welcomed with intelligent enthusiasm the first collection of Lermontov's poems, as well as his novel *A Hero of our Time*, both of which appeared in 1840. The poet had to thank this critic above all for a short cut to fame. Yet while Lermontov the poet could now look with satisfaction to the result of his work, Lermontov the man was surrounded by dangers, coming not so much from without as from the inner recesses of his own nature. Some of these proved to be his undoing.

6

His principal danger lay in his own divided personality. The contradictions with which he surprised so many of his acquaintances were not only in his character, but even in his appearance. Prince N. V. Lóbanov-Rostóvsky, for instance, who met Lermontov at St. Petersburg in 1838, describes him as 'ungainly to look at and small of stature, but he had a pleasant face and his eyes sparkled with intelligence. When tête-à-tête and outside the circle of his own comrades, he was an amiable fellow and his conversation was interesting, always original, though somewhat sarcastic. In his own circle, however, he was the very demon of turbulence, noise, scandal and scoffing. He simply could not live without pursuing some victim or other with ridicule.' [1]

Belínsky was often so shocked by the poet's character that he complained to the editor and writer Panáyev: 'I have not heard a single serious intelligent word from Lermontov. He seems to put on the superficiality of a man of the world.' Yet after a long talk with him in April 1840 (when the poet was under arrest) the same Belínsky exclaimed: 'What a fine tender soul of a poet!' Then he added as an afterthought: 'But I am sure he is already sorry for having shown me his true nature even for a moment.' [2]

This last remark comes very close to Lermontov's 'true nature'. He often seemed to indulge in unpleasant behaviour in order to hide, as well as to defy, what was good and kindly in himself. He could be two entirely different individuals with one and the same person, according to the mood of the moment. Thus in the spring of 1841, while in Moscow, he twice saw the young German poet Bodenstedt. The first impression he made on his German admirer and subsequent translator was highly unfavourable. But when the two saw each other again, Bodenstedt was charmed by his company.

[1] Originally written in French, Prince Lóbanov-Rostóvsky's *Memoirs* were published in Russian by the State Historical Museum. The above quotation is taken from *Lit. Naslédstvo* 54–56, p. 397.

[2] I. I. Panáyev, *Literatúrnye vospominánya* (*Literary Reminiscences*) pp. 136–7.

Of great interest is also Turgénev's description of the poet whom he saw (without speaking to him) at a society ball in the winter of 1840. 'In Lermontov's appearance there was something sinister and tragic,' he says in his *Literary Reminiscences*, 'a kind of dark and fatal strength, spiteful melancholy and a fervent passion imprinted on his swarthy face, in his big, dark and motionless eyes. Their heavy look formed a strange contrast to the expression of his slightly protruding lips which were tender like the lips of a child. His thickset frame, his bow-legs, big head, large shoulders and slightly bent figure made an unpleasant impression; still, one could not help feeling in him a certain power. . . . It is beyond any doubt that, following the fashion of the period, he had adopted a certain Byronic style seasoned with even worse whims and caprices of his own. But he paid a terrible penalty for them. It seems that in the depth of his heart Lermontov was profoundly bored. He felt stifled in the narrow sphere to which he had been relegated by fate.'

Unadaptable by his very nature, Lermontov was always in conflict with his own surroundings. He seemed to enjoy quarrels or misunderstandings, and even to look for them whatever the pretext. Thus in February 1840 he quarrelled at a ball with the son of the French ambassador and historian de Barante. The argument led to a duel in which Lermontov was slightly wounded. As the affair had aroused some

scandal, Lermontov was arrested and sent, once
again, to the Caucasus.

7

This time he took part in several expeditions
against the Caucasian mountaineers. As if
prompted by a secret death-wish, he showed
reckless daring in the skirmishes, but was spared
by the enemy bullets. His courage was com-
mended by the General in charge, but the powers-
that-be in far-off St. Petersburg paid no attention.
He was in utter disgrace.

As in 1837, the indefatigable Mme Arséneva
strained all her resources to get her grandson
back to the capital, but without success. Count
Benkendorf would no longer listen to her. The
Tsar himself, on reading *A Hero of our Time*, is
supposed to have referred to its author's 'de-
pravity', and this alone was enough to seal his
fate. Disgusted with it all, Lermontov now
thought of retiring from the army in order to
give all his time to literature. He spoke quite
seriously about it to Count Sollogúb and even
mentioned the possibility of editing a periodical
of his own. The authorities refused to release
him from the army but granted him a prolonged
leave towards the end of 1840. He was thus able
to spend the first three or four months of 1841
in St. Petersburg and partly in Moscow.

Late in the spring of 1841 he was again on his
way back to the Caucasus. When he and his gay

cousin 'Mongo' Stolýpin reached the fashionable Caucasian spa of Pyatigórsk, they found there several old acquaintances and decided to interrupt their journey. Among the companions Lermontov met in the spa was his one-time school-fellow Major Martýnov, whose sister Nadézhda had fallen in love with him (during his brief stay in Moscow), but was treated by him rather shabbily. For some inexplicable reason Lermontov began to pursue Major Martýnov with all the sarcasms he could think of. As the Major was something of a cheap romantic poseur, it was not difficult for the poet to mark him as a target for ridicule.

It seems that the Major entreated Lermontov to give up such provocative and indeed silly behaviour, but this only incensed his tormentor all the more. When the poet forgot himself to the extent of ridiculing his victim even in the presence of ladies in the house of the Cossack General Verzílin, Martýnov was obliged to challenge him to a duel. The duel took place on 27 July 1841 on the outskirts of Pyatigórsk. The two opponents met during a violent storm. Shots were exchanged to the accompaniment of lightning and thunder, and Lermontov was killed outright—in the twenty-seventh year of his life.

II

A Poet's Progress

I

As Lermontov is considered the greatest Russian poet after Pushkin it is not amiss to point out, from the outset, certain differences between the two poets both of whom started writing verse at a surprisingly early age. It is known that Pushkin, who had been brought up above all on French and classical culture, showed even in his first efforts an amazing skill and flair for the right word. Lermontov, however, belonged to the generation whose youth had been passed in a romantic literary climate, with all its emotional effusions. In fact, he himself had to struggle with these for quite a while before he reached the pregnant simplicity of his mature work—a process during which he kept returning to the same themes at different periods, until his artistic conscience was more or less satisfied with the result. Nor did he shrink from inserting entire passages from his earlier poems into later works, provided he could strengthen thereby the artistic texture and effect of the final product.

Lermontov's years of apprenticeship (roughly from 1828 until 1836) were imitative and until 1832 largely autobiographical. His early efforts which, incidentally, were not intended for print, abound in romantic motifs, figures, *clichés*, and antitheses (such as heaven and hell, angel and demon, etc.). They are also full of an exaggeratedly gloomy outlook upon life and the world. Yet even here one can feel Lermontov's musical and rhythmic sense combined with a surprising ease in versification. His sense of colour, too, served him well; and indeed he continued to sketch and to paint to the last days of his life. Furthermore, among his youthful outpourings one comes upon occasional flashes of genius which anticipate, as it were, the vigour of his mature phase. As for his exaggerated subjectivity, it is conspicuous first of all in his early love poems. These are, for the most part, records of his loves and disappointments, combined with a feeling of isolation which was not merely social: it went much deeper, despite its fashionable garb of the *mal du siècle*. His uprootedness in the world even acquired a kind of metaphysical flavour which is best expressed in one of his well-known poems *Angel* (*The Angel*), written at the age of sixteen and beginning with the line, *Po nébu polúnochi ángel letél*. As we shall have to refer to this poem later on, it is rendered here in an English version—however inadequate.

An angel flew through the midnight sky
And gently he sang on high.
And the moon, and the stars, and the clouds in
    a throng
Were entranced by that holy song.

'He sang of the bliss of the souls without sin
The heavenly tents within.
Of great God he sang, and all the while
His praise was pure, without guile.

A young soul he carried in his embrace
To this world of grief and disgrace;
And the wordless song he sang on the way
In the young soul then echoed for aye.

And during the long years allotted to her
She was full of a wondrous despair,
And the tedious songs of this world would in
    vain
Try to silence that heavenly strain.

The autobiographical element comes out also
in Lermontov's dramatic writings and in his
prose. A true romantic by temperament, but
deprived very early of any romantic faith, he
tended to develop even in his youthful works,
alongside the 'purple patches' and emotional
intensity, a rather cool judgment and an aggres-
sively sarcastic manner. If the first of these two
inclinations fed at times on the 'furious' French
romantics then in vogue, the second must have
drawn encouragement from Byron as well as
from the writings of such a shrewd observer as
La Rochfoucauld and other French *moralistes* of
his stamp. This contrast between an essentially
romantic nature and a cool realistic thinker or
observer comes out in Lermontov's style, or

rather in his two styles, which are typical even of the works written during the last phase of his life. Yet quite apart from any stylistic considerations, one cannot help feeling a great deal of energy and vitality even in his immature writings. As Belínsky wrote in a letter to his friend Bótkin: 'All this may be juvenile, but it is terribly strong and dynamic. A lion-like character. A formidable and powerful spirit.'

Lermontov never lost this 'terribly strong and dynamic' quality. It increased, if anything, with the years. But before reaching his full stature as a poet, he had to experience certain phases and influences, mention of which is imperative in a sketch of his literary growth.

2

There were three writers in particular whose impact on Lermontov's early poetry was strong indeed: Pushkin, Byron, and the Schiller of the 'storm and stress' (*Sturm und Drang*) period. The interaction of these influences often determined the themes and the very character of his works at that stage. As for his Byronic tales in verse, they were originally suggested to him by Pushkin's 'southern poems', Zhukóvsky's excellent translation of *The Prisoner of Chillon*, and also Kozlóv's Russian version of *The Bride of Abydos*. The *Kavkázskiy plénnik* (*The Prisoner of the Caucasus*), in which Pushkin introduced into Russian literature the disappointed Childe Harold type, Lermontov simply rewrote in his own way at the age of fourteen, and retained Pushkin's own title. But whereas young Pushkin soon overcame (and even debunked) the isolated and self-absorbed Byronic egoist, Lermontov was himself too much of a *déraciné* by nature to give up such a character. Having modified him instead, he gave a magnificent symbol of his predicament in *The Demon*, and its psychological analysis in his novel, *A Hero of our Time*.

It should be stressed, though, that his early Byronic tales in verse were mainly in the nature of poetic exercises. At the same time Byron helped to intensify and perhaps also to clarify some of those features which were latent in Lermontov from the beginning. It was not mere fashion but a case of genuine affinity with the English poet which made Lermontov exclaim (at the age of fifteen) that, sharing 'Byron's soul and sounds' he would like to share also his fate. He was flattered by any resemblance he found between Byron and himself.[1] Yet at the same time he stressed his own independence even in one of his early poems, beginning with the words, *Ya ne Byron, ya drugóy* (I am not Byron, but someone else).

It goes without saying that he was strongly drawn also towards Pushkin. But here the attraction was due mainly to the law of contrasts,

---

[1] He also translated Byron's *Farewell*, *My Soul is Dark*, while the motif of his *Dying Gladiator* (1836) was taken from the fourth Canto of *Childe Harold*.

since the two poets were utterly different in their attitudes towards life and the world. Even the texture of Lermontov's poems differs from that of Pushkin's. In Pushkin it is each individual word that counts, for he knows how to derive from it its full poetic value. Lermontov's poetry, on the other hand, is distinguished by the musical and rhythmic flow of the line much more than by the choice of words. In this he is nearer to Zhukóvsky than to Pushkin. Even in those mature poems in which he achieved the crystalline simplicity of Pushkin's verse, he retained a texture and an 'accent' entirely his own.

Nor was Lermontov's interest in Schiller negligible. The pathos and impetus of Schiller's early plays appealed to him on account of their note of protest. He also translated some of Schiller's poems: *Der Handschuh* (*The Glove*) for instance, *An Emma* (*To Emma*) and *Die Begegnung* (*The Encounter*). Later he came across another German poet, Heinrich Heine, in whom he found a somewhat kindred nature. Both Lermontov and Heine were endowed with similar emotional intensity, and also hidden sentimentality which they tried to camouflage under the cover of flippancy and jeering irony. Scratch Heine's flippancy, and you will find under it a wounded or frustrated idealist. The same holds good of Lermontov. Finally, Heine—like Lermontov—had been jilted by his beloved, who married another and thus left a scar in the poet's heart for the rest of his life. As for other influences, Lermontov was familiar with Lamartine, de Musset, and especially with Victor Hugo whose *Les Orientales* caused considerable stir among the romantics of the period. There are some surmises that he must have known and read with profit also the works of the great Polish poet Adam Mickiewicz. Yet none of these influences can be compared with that of Byron's.

It was not only Byron the poet but Byron the rebel that appealed to his Russian admirer. And so did the defiant and self-willed characters in Byron's tales in verse. As Lermontov too, like Byron, was addicted to self-dramatization, he soon began to identify himself with a series of romantic rebels whom he depicted preferably against the Caucasian background—a fitting substitute for the 'Eastern' background in Byron's early tales. There were plenty of picturesque or 'mysterious' outlaws among the Caucasian mountaineers, and young Lermontov found it easy to weave fantastic plots around them, without trying to disguise his indebtedness to Byron. What he wanted to achieve in and through those exercises was such technical ability as would give him confidence in his own talent. This was one of the reasons why, during his years of apprenticeship, he also experimented with drama and prose. A cursory glance at his plays might illustrate some further interesting aspects of that experimental period.

His two earliest plays, *Ispántsy* (*The Spaniards*), in blank verse, and *Menschen und Leidenschaften* (*Men and Passions*)[1], go back to 1830, when the poet was not more than sixteen. A year later he wrote his autobiographical melodrama *Stránny chelovék* (*A Queer Fellow*). His two maturer plays *Maskarád* (*The Masked Ball*), in four-footed and five-footed rhymed iambics, and *Dva Bráta* (*The Two Brothers*) were written in 1835 and 1836 respectively.

Like Byron, Lermontov knows one hero only whom he projects again and again into his main characters, namely himself. However juvenile and declamatory he may be at times, he is yet skilful at handling melodramatic situations in the 'furious' romantic style. The impact of Schiller's *Die Räuber* (*The Brigands*) and *Kabale und Liebe* (*Chicane and Love*) is here obvious. Besides, Lermontov saw a memorable performance of both plays on the Moscow stage with the famous actor Kachálov in the main roles. Another stimulus may have come from Victor Hugo's *Hernani*, whose literary *succès de scandale* reverberated even in far-off Russia. Yet for all his declamatory propensities he began to pay more and more attention to the pointed dialogue. In his last two plays, for instance, especially in *The Masked Ball*,

[1] Lermontov himself gave it, for reasons unknown, its German title.

one finds a number of passages which are tersely sententious and epigrammatic.

These summary remarks can now be completed by a few references to individual plays. *The Spaniards*, for example, is reminiscent not only of Schiller but also of Lessing's *Nathan der Weise* (*Nathan the Wise*)—minus the happy ending in Lessing's humanitarian play. At the same time it is typical of an 'angry young man' of the period. Here Lermontov not only attacks religious persecution, but definitely takes sides and defends the oppressed—in this case the Spanish Jews.

His next two plays, *Menschen und Leidenschaften* and *A Queer Fellow*, are largely personal. The first of them reflects the family quarrels between Mme Arséneva and Lermontov's father (on account of the boy's education), whereas the second is in essence a self-portrait of Lermontov against the Moscow background. Its principal character, Arbénin, is obviously the author himself—in the process of squaring his accounts with one of his former loves (Nadya Ivánova). It is also a drama of isolation. Incidentally, it contains a violent protest against the serfdom system, the abuses of which Lermontov could witness on his grandmother's estate.

These three plays are purely experimental works. They represent Lermontov's quest for self-expression in the form of drama. *The Two Brothers*, on the other hand, is more mature, though not devoid either of literary reminiscences or of personal allusions. The antagonism of the

two brothers is akin to that between Karl and
Franz in Schiller's *Die Räuber*. It also contains a
camouflaged dramatic rendering of Lermontov's
encounter (in Moscow) with Várya and her
husband in December 1835, when he was on his
way to Tarkhány. The 'furious' dialogue of this
play jars on the modern reader. Yet it contains a
fair amount of that psychological flair which is
evident in *The Masked Ball*. In this drama or
melodrama of jealousy Lermontov emulates the
sententious rhymed verse of Griboyédov's play,
Góre ot umá (*Woe from Wit*).[1] As Griboyédov did
in that play, Lermontov here gives a satirical
picture of Russian high society. In many respects the play is also a modern transcription of
Shakespeare's *Othello*.

Its hero, Arbénin, is a dissipated young man
who, through the love of his young wife, Nina,
has become a reformed character. One night
Nina goes to a masked ball, where she loses her
brooch. The brooch is picked up by another
woman, who gives it to her lover—Arbénin's
friend. During a conversation with his friend,
Arbénin recognizes Nina's brooch, and this (like
Desdemona's handkerchief in *Othello*) unleashes
all his suspicions. The inner storm and chaos
aroused by his jealousy makes him kill his
innocent wife and lands him in madness.

Such was this play which Lermontov had

[1] I am using the title of the English version by Professor Pares. The literal translation of the Russian title
is *The Misfortune of Being Clever*.

written with an eye to the stage. He definitely wanted it to be performed, but the censors said *no*: partly because of the 'immorality' of the play, and partly because of the malicious picture of St. Petersburg society. In order to mollify the censors, Lermontov rewrote the play and called it simply *Arbénin*. In this second (and weaker) version Nina is actually guilty. But instead of killing her, Arbénin only abandons her with scorn. Even so *The Masked Ball* was not allowed to see the stage for some time. Its first performance took place in 1862—twenty-one years after its author's death.[1]

There can be no doubt that Arbénin belongs to the stock-in-trade romantic characters with a stormy past, and also with a 'demoniacal' strain in them which eventually prevails over their will or reason. His tragedy of jealousy is, on the whole, well handled. And so is the plot, with its tense atmosphere sustained from beginning to end.

4

Whatever the value of Lermontov's excursions into drama, they helped him resolve a number of rancorous moods and frustrations. They also contributed a great deal to his grasp of human character which came out in *A Hero of our Time*. But before reaching that stage he made some

[1] There exists also an interesting, though perhaps too lavish, Soviet film version of the play.

experiments with prose, too, as if determined not to neglect a single literary medium.

Lermontov's earliest attempts at writing prose go as far back as his Military School period. His unfinished novel *Vadím* was presumably written during 1833–34.[1] Obviously inspired by Sir Walter Scott on the one hand, and by Victor Hugo's *Notre Dame de Paris* on the other, this narrative is connected with the Pugachóv rebellion in the Urals which Pushkin later depicted in *Kapitánskaya dóchka* (*A Captain's Daughter*, 1836). But in contrast to Pushkin's classical realism Lermontov's story is romantic both in style and conception. Its chief character, Vadím, is a dispossessed and deformed nobleman—a kind of 'demoniacal' Quasimodo in a Russian setting. Full of rancorous frustrations, he sides with the Cossack rebels and, having turned against his own class, becomes one of their leaders. Did Lermontov intend to vent thereby his own social 'inferiority complex' as well as his hatred of those who refused to accept him as their equal? Be this as it may, the novel is the work of a talented beginner, and nothing more.

Entirely different is Lermontov's next novel *Knyagínya Ligovskáya* (*Princess Ligovskáya*), also unfinished and written in 1836. Devoid of

[1] The exact date is still somewhat uncertain. The manuscript of this novel was discovered in 1873 and was printed in the same year in *Véstnik Evrópy* (*The European Messenger*). Some of its portions were probably written by his friend S. A. Rayévsky.

rhetoric, its tone and manner are studiously realistic and confined to essentials. The action, which takes place in the Russian capital in the 1830's, has as its protagonists two contrasted characters. One of them is the social snob Pechórin, and the other the *déclassé* nobleman and minor official Krasínski. Both contain features typical of Lermontov himself. Pechórin is a priggish, coldly reasoning dandy whose view of society is realistic to the point of cynicism. Krasínski, on the other hand, is (like Lermontov) a petty nobleman by birth, but with the ambition to rise in the world to as high a level as possible. Pechórin's treatment of Negúrova is based on the unsavoury revenge Lermontov took on his one-time love Sushkóva after having met her in St. Petersburg. As for the Princess and her elderly husband, they are transparent allusions to Várya after her marriage to Bakhmétyev—this story was written practically at the same time as *The Two Brothers*.

In *Princess Ligovskáya* we have the Petersburg of Gogol's *Nevsky Prospect* and *The Diary of a Madman*. The society ball as described by Lermontov is actually reminiscent of the ball in *Nevsky Prospect*. Yet Lermontov's language, in contrast to Gogol's, is here sober and analytical. Although still far from being perfect, this narrative represents, as it were, a prelude to *A Hero of our Time*, which was completed some three or four years later. Before passing again to Lermontov the poet we ought to mention his *Ashík-*

Keríb, a well-told paraphrase of a Tartar folk-tale which he must have heard in 1837. It testifies to his interest in the East and Eastern folklore, which he tried to assimilate during his roamings in the Caucasus.

5

While experimenting with drama and prose, Lermontov showed a decreased output in both lyrical and narrative poetry. Thus in 1832 he finished only one tale in verse—*Ismaíl-Bey*; another, *Hadji Abrék*, during 1833–1834, and one again *Boyárin Órsha* (*The Boyar Orsha*) during the next two years.

The favourite character of his juvenile romantic tales is of course the mysterious and unadaptable Byronic hero. Love, crime, jealousy, revenge—they all abound in them, as in Byron's Eastern tales. Nor is Byron's love of freedom and rebellion forgotten. It is more than transparent even in *Poslédniy syn vólnosti* (*The Last Son of Liberty*), a tale in verse about Nóvgorod's resistance to the Viking invaders in the ninth century, which Lermontov wrote in 1830—at the age of sixteen. It took a number of years though before he brought this genre to the height of perfection in *The Novice* and in the final version of *The Demon*.

Lermontov's first work to be printed (against his will) was *Hadji Abrék*,[1] a romantic tale of

[1] It appeared in Senkóvski's *Bibliotéka dlya chténiya* (*Library for Reading*), 1835.

vengeful killing and being killed, told with considerable artistic economy. A further step towards such concentration was made by him in *The Boyar Órsha*, which will be discussed later. And so will his 'realistic' tales in verse: *Tambóvskaya Kaznachéisha* (*A Treasurer's Wife from Tambov*), *Sáshka* and *Skázka dlya detéy* (*A Tale for Children*). These three belong to Lermontov's last period in which were produced not only such masterpieces as *The Novice*, *The Demon* and *A Hero of our Time*, but also the finest of his lyrics. In order to see these works in their right perspective one should first give a definition of Lermontov's romanticism as it manifested itself in his life and his work.

III

Lermontov and the Romantic Mind

I

The trouble with romanticism is that it means so many things and can be approached from so many angles. A number of its facets may look contradictory or even incompatible, at least on the surface. The important thing however is to find out what they have in common rather than where they differ.

The rise of European romanticism shows, on the whole, two main stages, each of them dominated by a mood of its own. Whereas the mood, as well as the impetus, of the first stage had been one of liberation, the second stage was imbued with disillusionment and frustration. What both phases had in common was, of course, their protest against the existing pattern of life. Rousseau, the German 'storm and stress' (*Sturm und Drang*) group, the ideologists of the French Revolution—they all were animated by their wish to destroy what they regarded as obsolete, even when their ideals of a new life were either too vague or too utopian. Still, they believed in those ideals.

Not so the representatives of the second and more important wave of the romantic tide. The

47

bankruptcy of the Revolution on the one hand, and the meanness of the triumphant emerging bourgeoisie on the other, had a sobering effect on the more sensitive minds in Europe. The disillusionment was all the greater because of the excessive hopes which had preceded it. The new post-revolutionary generation, whatever its romantic leanings, was thus stripped at the outset of practically all romantic faith. Hence their gloomy *Weltschmerz* or *mal du siècle*, usually accompanied by a challenge to the new society with its cash-and-credit system. *Épatez le bourgeois* soon became the slogan of the frustrated young romantics who—in true bohemian fashion —turned, or were ready to turn, against all bourgeois cant and conventions, the respectable bourgeois morality included. At the same time they often paraded not only their own exceptional tastes, manners (or the lack of them) and emotions, but even their exceptional vices—in fact anything that could sustain their idea of being different from ordinary 'bourgeois' mortals. Such at any rate was the path of romantic defiance.

There were however a number of more passive and feminine characters who preferred the path of escape. Estranged as they were from the life around, they tried to ignore or forget it in a number of ways. Nature-worship, whether in its 'maternal', pantheistic, sentimental or purely aesthetic appeal, was one of them. Another shelter from the hated present was offered by an idealized and intensely picturesque past. Hence the vogue of Sir Walter Scott all over Europe.[1] There were romantics who dreamed of feudal, or Catholic-feudal, restorations. Others turned towards an idealized utopian future. Some further escapes were provided by aesthetic 'ivory towers', by all sorts of imaginary adventures, or by amorous and sentimental–idyllic romances full of wishful thinking. Also, religious and mystical inclinations became the fashion of the day, not to mention the prodigious number of converts to Roman Catholicism during the romantic period. And since in the eyes of a romantic the objective, finite reality was discredited, a flight into the infinite or the Absolute gained in its philosophic appeal. So did that intense subjectivism and interest in man's inner world, a valuable by-product of which is our modern analytical or psychological novel.

Nor should one omit a third group of romantics: those who felt frustrated in the actual world but preferred to go back to it rather than away from it. They went back to the hated reality in order to expose it in all its nakedness and thus avenge their own estrangement from life. And the more romantic the feeling of uprootedness behind such an impulse, the more realistic were

[1] Yet among the politically enslaved nations, such as the Poles, the Czechs, etc., the nostalgic revival of the past, fostered by the historical novel, fanned also the spark of that patriotism which kept the hope of a national liberation alive.

their descriptions of the life which they wanted to discredit. Here we actually touch upon the borderline where romanticism passes into realism by adopting the latter's methods. There are a number of such crypto-romantics among European writers: from Flaubert and Gogol to Thomas Hardy. One should bear in mind, though, that no romantic is endowed with only one of the above-mentioned features. One usually finds a few of them together. It all depends on which of them prevails.

2

The question arises where Russian romanticism comes in and what was Lermontov's contribution to it. In dealing with this problem one should remember first of all that the stock-in-trade of romantic themes and moods was more or less the same all over Europe, although each nation gave them a garb and 'inflection' of its own. It is in this sense only that one can speak of an English, French, German, Russian or Polish type of romanticism. In Russia the somewhat belated romantic movement drew its inspiration above all from England and from Germany. Zhukóvsky's fine translation (in 1802) of Gray's *Elegy* is often regarded as the first step in that direction which in the 1820's culminated in the impact of Byron upon Russian poetry and in the 1830's in that of Sir Walter Scott upon Russian prose.

As for German influences, the idealistic philosophy of Schelling should be mentioned first. The 'Wisdom Lovers', grouped in the 1820's around the talented young poet Dmitry Venevítinov (1805–27), were particularly interested in Schelling. A number of subsequent Slavophils (Khomyakóv, the brothers Kiréyevsky, etc.) were among them. Also the hauntingly pantheistic poetry of Fëdor Tyútchev, who made his debut in 1836–37, bears the imprint of Schelling's *Naturphilosophie*. After Schelling (and partly Fichte) there came the influence of Hegel. The conversion of the critic Belínsky from Schelling to Hegel and to left-wing Hegelianism affected not only Belínsky himself, but, to a large extent, the ideological structure of Russian intelligentsia who derived some of their main tenets precisely from him.

Yet the classical eighteenth-century tradition lingered on in Russia longer than in some other countries. When in his *The Prisoner of the Caucasus* (1821) Pushkin introduced the uprooted Childe Harold type to Russian readers, he avoided romantic exuberance. This tale in verse is written with economy and with that poetic realism which was to reach its high-water mark in his 'novel in verse' *Evgény Onégin*—a work in which the fashionable Byronic poseur was debunked as a 'Muscovite in Childe Harold's cloak', but in a thoroughly Russian setting. Something new was brought into Russian literature by Gogol's romantic stories (in the early 1830's), redolent of folklore, and told in that ornate and agitated language which was so different from the prose of Pushkin. In his novel *Dead Souls* (1842), written in the same agitated style, Gogol again produced a masterpiece of that realism of indictment which can be defined as romanticism in reverse.

It is known that Belínsky founded his theory of the 'natural school' largely on Gogol's so-called realism. He demanded not only that the writers should depict 'natural', i.e. ordinary people and ordinary life, but that they should also expose all the evils of life in the name of a better and worthier existence. The majority of subsequent Russian realists accepted Belínsky's principal tenets, including the element of indictment. Another romantic aspect absorbed by Russian realism was the Onégin-like *déraciné* turned into a thoroughly Russian 'superfluous man' and shown as a product of Russian conditions. But before this happened, it was Lermontov above all who reached in his work the very climax of Russian romanticism and at the same time paved the way for the Russian realists as well. No one before him had given a more intense expression to that state of social and spiritual uprootedness or isolation which, later on, played such an important part in a series of 'superfluous men' from Turgénev's Rúdin and Goncharóv's Oblómov to Dostoévsky's Stavrógin (in *The Possessed*), not to mention a galaxy of Chekhov's 'superfluous' characters.

3

The feeling of isolation clung to Lermontov from his early boyhood. Whether he was unable or else unwilling to adjust himself to his surroundings, the result was much the same: the awareness of being an exile in his own country. This was perhaps one of the reasons why he was so fond of the Caucasian scenery. In the majesty of those landscapes he could forget himself and thus ease the burden of his loneliness. But once back among human beings, he found again and again how little real contact he had with them. He may have been on the look-out for conflicts and quarrels simply in order to stifle for a while the same oppressive feeling of isolation. In one of his well-known poems, *Párus* (*The Sail*), he compares himself with a lone white sail tossed by the sea and all the time looking for storms 'as if in storms alone were peace'.

Yet the more isolated such an individual feels among other human beings the more is he likely to assert himself against them. He is also inclined to see in his very isolation a proof of his own exclusiveness and superiority. As a pretence of this kind is never devoid of secret doubts, he will often be tempted to display his superiority in terms of defiant exhibitionism. Extravagant dress, so typical of some romantic bohemians, was however less harmful in this respect than their extravagant attitudes towards the accepted values of good and evil. In their rancour against life and the world they adopted at times even the cult of evil decked in 'demoniac' or 'satanic' trappings. Yet a pose of this kind was often combined with something more sinister. Such at least was the case of Lermontov who was continually haunted by the symbolic image of the 'demon'. Belínsky once said that whereas Pushkin avoided meeting his own 'demon' (although he was familiar with him), Lermontov welcomed such encounters and revelled in them. Even as a youth he confessed in one of his poems to being 'like my own demon an elect of evil'.

The romantic cult of evil can be fostered not only by the elation derived from one's negative sense of power, but also by the feeling of 'damnation' the painful intensity of which is itself regarded as a privilege. There exists in fact such a thing as the snobbery of suffering. Verlaine's label of *les poètes maudits* was meant to be a distinction rather than a reproach. Like Leopardi, Baudelaire, Dostoévsky and Nietzshe, Lermontov identified the intensity of life above all with the intensity of pain. And since great pain was in his eyes an advantage, he was on the look-out for it and welcomed it as a proof of his own exclusiveness. He was only seventeen when he exclaimed in his autobiographic poem *11 June 1831*: 'I want to love and I pray to heaven for new torments.'

He had his share of torments. But these only sharpened his indignation on the one hand and his appetite for pain on the other. And since he found a number of pretexts for being indignant also with the political and social conditions of his own country, his personal resentment was increased by his anger as a citizen. Jointly they caused him to write verses in the tradition of that 'Decembrist' poetry which had been muzzled, though not strangled, after the December revolt in 1825. In some of his poems of indictment it is difficult to say where one ends and the other begins.

Lermontov certainly did not mince words in *The Death of a Poet*. His *Dúma* (*Meditation*, 1838) is another scathing poem of the same kind. Here are some of the indictments he hurled in it at his contemporaries: 'We are rich from our very cradle in the errors and belated understanding of our fathers, and life wearies us like a level road without a destination, or like a drawn-out banquet. Shamelessly indifferent to good and evil, we wilt without a struggle at the outset of our career. We are disgracefully pusillanimous in danger and despicable slaves when faced by might.' [1] The list of other vices, too, was long enough to serve as a warning for young Russian intellectuals of any period. A contemptuous on-slaught on high society proper is contained how-ever in the poem beginning with 'How frequently

[1] This poem, written *pro domo*, may have been origin-ally suggested to Lermontov by *Le campo Vaccino* whose author, Henri Auguste Barbier—now almost forgotten—was a well-known French satirical poet of the day.

amidst a motley crowd' and dated *1 January 1840*.
Here his civic indignation is duly strengthened
by his personal rancour, and vice versa.

Yet whatever his attacks, they were devoid of
that faith which alone might have taken him outside and beyond his own ego. Incurably self-
absorbed, this romantic yet remained at the
mercy of his cold and sceptical mind which
showed him only the price but not the value of
things. As Alexander Herzen put it in his
French pamphlet, *Du mouvement des idées revolu-
tionnaires en Russie*: 'Lermontov never learned
how to hope and never sacrificed his own self,
since nothing demanded of him such a sacrifice.
He did not walk onto the scaffold with a proudly
lifted head like Péstel and Ryléyev, because he
did not believe in the reality of such a sacrifice;
he stood aside of truth and perished without
rhyme or reason.'

However severe Herzen's verdict may sound,
it was not Lermontov's fault that he could never
bridge the gap in his own divided personality.
Romantic by his nature and sceptical by his mind,
he was doomed to suffer from that painful inner
dichotomy the like of which one finds in no
other Russian poet except the symbolist Alexander Blok—in many respects a modern counterpart of Lermontov.[1] No wonder Lermontov ex-
perienced the whole of life in terms of antinomies

[1] It is not without interest that Alexander Blok himself felt his inner affinity with Lermontov and was enthusiastic about his work.

and contradictions. Tossed between these, he was inconsistent even where his fundamental impulses (his love of freedom, for instance) were concerned.

It is known that he sincerely sympathized with the Caucasian tribes fighting for their liberty. Yet he opened the third Canto of his *Ismail Bey* with this paean to the encroaching Russian invaders: 'Resign, Circassian! East and West will share, perhaps quite soon, your own fate. A time will come when you will humbly say, "Slave though I am, I serve the master of the world!"' Even more ambiguous is his poem *Spor* (*Argument*), written during the last months of his life. Here Lermontov uses the language of one who condones Russian aggressive designs in the whole of the Middle East as a kind of historical fatality. When on his way back to the Caucasus in April 1841, he stopped in Moscow and took the poem to the young Slavophil Samárin whom he asked to give it to the editor of the *Moskvityánin* (*The Muscovite*)—the last periodical anyone could have accused of liberal, let alone seditious, tendencies.

A further proof of Lermontov's split personality is provided by his attitude towards love. One of his two lyrics under the title *Molítva* (*Prayer*), in which he appeals to the Holy Virgin to protect his sweetheart, is among the tenderest love poems in the Russian language. Yet at the same time he was able to write unprintable 'barracks' verses and to treat women like a mere voluptuary. Still, it was through his apparent flippancy that he often vented his disgust with life as he saw it. The bitter irony of such tales in verse as his *A Treasurer's Wife* and *Sáshka*, is a case in point. The grin one finds in them is the grin of a wounded idealist anxious to cover up his own wounds.

4

A Treasurer's Wife reads like an anecdote of drab provincial existence. It is written in the *Onégin*-stanzas (fourteen lines of four-footed iambics), and its flippant tone is only a camouflage for the poet's romantic disgust with life as he found it.

The reader is taken to a remote provincial town whose elderly treasurer is married to a pretty young wife, but, being a miser and a gambler in one, does not waste his time on amorous occupations. Unexpectedly a regiment of soldiers arrives. The dashing young officer who is billetted opposite the treasurer's house, soon gets a sight of his pretty vis-à-vis. Nor is the bored young woman unaware of her new neighbour, although she sees him mostly from the distance. Having caught his wife and the officer alone in his house, the treasurer does not think of the customary duel. He invites his rival to a gambling party instead. Anxious to empty the Captain's pockets, the treasurer takes the game in all earnest. The contest drags on through the night at the end of which the host has gambled away to his opponent not only all his money but everything he possesses. In a fit of frenzy he finally stakes his wife and loses. Having watched the proceedings, the young woman pulls her wedding-ring from her finger, flings it at her husband, and swoons into the arms of her new owner, who takes her to his quarters.

Even more incisive in its sardonic realism is the partly autobiographic but unfinished *Sáshka* (1839).[1] It consists of only two chapters. They read like the beginning of another 'novel in verse' and also make one think of certain passages in Byron's *Don Juan*. Lermontov chose for his hero a dissipated young dandy who visits a little house occupied by two prostitutes on the outskirts of Moscow. The visitor, the two dames and their setting are depicted in the style of a 'connoisseur'. One of the prostitutes suddenly has the bright idea that she would like to be taken (properly disguised) by her cavalier to an exclusive society ball. The dandy, much amused, promises to fulfil her whim. And here the tale ends.

The impression it gives is that of a fragment. Whether or not the poet intended to continue it, is difficult to say. As it stands, it strikes one as much by its sureness of touch as by the grim laughter of a romantic who relishes his revenge upon life. One of Sáshka's reminiscences dwelt upon is his love for a pretty serf-girl who was later raped by his own father.

[1] The Russian diminutive of Alexander. Lermontov borrowed the title from a notorious poem by Alexander Polezháyev.

Lermontov left one more realistic tale in verse —also unfinished—under the rather misleading title of *Skázka dlya detéy* (*A Tale for Children*). It is one of his best things, but as it is connected with his ever-recurring Demon-motif, it will be discussed in the next chapter.

5

There is no need to stress the fact that Lermontov's protest and realism of indictment were but two further aspects of a romantic who knew what to rebel against and yet was never quite sure what to rebel for. Even his passion for freedom became insufficient, at least in so far as freedom demands some positive scope or contents to be filled with in order not to become sterile.

Lermotov, the man and the poet, was fully aware of this. In one of his poignant lyrics, written in 1837, he refers to his 'dread of the days to come' and compares himself to a criminal who, before execution, looks around in vain for a kindred soul in order to ease his own loneliness. Referring to his inner travail, the poet says that he himself is waiting for a new life. But this new life was slow in coming. For one thing, Lermontov was too much of a romantic to give up that pain and suffering the 'exclusiveness' of which he regarded as a kind of personal distinction. On the other hand, the sceptic in him was much too honest to accept on credit any remedy which might have taken him out of his own

60

predicament. But when the predicament itself (with all its implications) became unbearable, he had to try to overcome it one way or the other.

Actually, there remained for him only two ways of dealing with it: either to deepen his own loneliness and frustration into an inner tragedy expressed with all the poetic power at his disposal; or else to analyse them away as a malady one has to face whatever the consequences. The first he did in his two narrative poems, *The Novice* and *The Demon*; and the second, in his novel, *A Hero of our Time*. These three works bring us to the very peak of Lermontov's creative efforts and achievements.

IV

The Climax

I

It was not by accident that Lermontov completed his two masterpieces, *The Novice* and *The Demon*, only towards the end of his brief life. The fact that he had been preoccupied with both for years before they took their final shape proves that he was anxious to put into them something that was of vital importance to himself. And in this he fully succeeded. Hence their intensity and the pleasure they still give one despite the passage of time.

Like Byron's tale in verse *The Prisoner of Chillon*, *The Novice* too is a poetic monologue. It is written in the energetic four-footed iambics which Zhukóvsky used in his fine translation (1821) of Byron's poem. Apart from the introduction, the whole of *The Novice* is a confession (not unlike the monk's confession in Byron's *Giaour*) in which rhythm, phrasing and diction are saturated with an unflagging dynamic quality from the first to the last line.

The poem itself was finished in 1839, but its genesis goes at least as far back as 1830. The earliest highly romantic draft, called simply *Íspoved* (*A Confession*), is set in a dungeon where a young monk, guilty of a sinful love-affair with a nun, is waiting to be led to the scaffold there to expiate his crime. A decrepit grey-haired monk enters the dungeon and exhorts the culprit to repent before it is too late. But, instead of the expected repentance the youth confesses, in defiant terms, his love of life, of freedom and of the beauty of the world. Ready to pay the price for the ecstasy of his illicit love, he is indifferent to the torments of the execution.

More complicated was Lermontov's next attempt to present the same theme. The poet interpolated it in the second part of his tale in verse, *The Boyar Órsha*. This time the setting is the boyar's estate near the Lithuanian border in the days of Ivan the Terrible. The boyar's beautiful daughter is in love with one of her father's retainers—the commoner Arsény. The two lovers are caught in the girl's room at night by the old boyar himself. The angry father locks his daughter in her room and throws the key into the river below. As for Arsény, he is delivered to the monks of the monastery near by for trial and execution. At the trial, which takes place in the boyar's presence, the ascetic blind prior of the monastery makes no impression on the prisoner, whose mood is not one of regret. On the contrary, he flings at his judges one challenge after the other even in the face of death. On the night before the execution Arsény escapes to Lithuania, where he gathers a band of outlaws and becomes their leader. In due course he invades the vast territory of the boyar, who is mortally wounded. Asked by Arsény as to the whereabouts of his daughter, the dying boyar tells him where to find her. Arsény hurries to Orsha's palace. He forces his way into the locked room, but all he finds is the skull and the bleached bones of the girl once so dear to him.

Evidently not pleased with this version either, Lermontov took up the motif once more when he was at the height of his creative power. The background now chosen was the Caucasus. A lucky chance provided the requisite subject-matter. In the autumn 1837, while on the way to his first Caucasian exile, Lermontov had stopped in the one-time Georgian capital Mtskheti, where he was shown a semi-deserted monastery guarded by an old monk—its last and only inmate. It was from this monk that Lermontov heard the story which he later turned into the narrative poem known as *The Novice*.

The monk told him how as a boy he had been captured in his native mountains by the Russians, who wanted to take him to their own country. But on the way he fell ill and was left with the monks of that monastery. The monks nursed the boy back to health and let him stay on. Thus he became a novice whose world was reduced to the narrow monastery walls. But the memory of his free life in the mountains haunted him day and night. And so did the nostalgia for his native village. He found his prison-like existence in the monastery so intolerable that he escaped. In the hope of reaching his *aoól* (village) he wandered in the forest until he lost his way. Starved and utterly weary, he was found by the searching monks, who brought him back to his cell. The futility of his flight made him decide to stay in the monastery, where he had remained ever since.

2

This adventure must have appealed to Lermontov's imagination. But he did not take up the monk's tale literally. He concentrated all his poetic power upon the novice's flight, as well as upon the scenery in which it took place, leaving out the resignation with which the recaptured fugitive stayed on in the monastery. The poem thus embodied the most spirited bid for freedom in Russian literature at a time when the very word 'freedom' was banned. Besides, the novice's adventures in the virgin forest were exciting enough to make the censor overlook what was 'between the lines' in this poem.

Seeing no difference between a monastery and a cage, the rebellious novice was ready to brave all the hazards of flight to regain his liberty. His adventures lasted only some three days, each crowded with risks and perils. One night he even met a starved panther, which he fought and killed with no stronger weapon than his club. His fight with the brute is described with such poetic realism as to be rightly placed among the finest passages Lermontov ever wrote.[1]

After three days and nights of roving, the novice realized that he was as far as ever from his goal. Finally he came, in a roundabout way, back to the haunts of the same 'cage' from which he had tried to escape. The sound of the familiar church-bell heard from afar left no doubt as to what had happened: instead of gaining freedom he had only moved in a circle. His passionate impulse had thus ended in frustration. Exhausted, he fell to the ground and regained consciousness only when back in his cell again. The monks, who had been looking for him, had picked him up and brought him to the monastery in a dying condition. He knew that life was now ebbing away, yet he refused to whine or to surrender to his fate. While talking to his father-confessor, he told him all about his adventures as well as about the reasons for his escape. His only regret was that his flight to life and freedom had been abortive. Although defeated, the novice thus remained defiant to the end. The poem contains no overt political allusions. But many a reader must have identified the novice's 'cage' with the political cage of Lermontov's Russia.

[1] There is another intense description of a fight between a man and a panther in the early thirteenth-century Georgian epic, *The Knight in the Panther Skin*, by Shóta Rustavéli—a contemporary of the famous queen Tamara. Not knowing Georgian, Lermontov could not have read this epic. He might have heard of it, though, from his Caucasian friends.

3

Another piece of defiance and frustration, but on a different plane, is Lermontov's best-known tale in verse, *The Demon*. The Demon himself as depicted by the poet is a symbol of metaphysical rebellion on the one hand and of cosmic isolation on the other. In spite of this, or perhaps because of it, it gives away as it were one of Lermontov's secrets and is perhaps more closely connected with his nature than anything else he wrote. Little wonder that he worked upon this tale in verse for years, persistently taking it up again and again. Its first draft was jotted down in 1829, when Lermontov was only fifteen. He finished it in 1838, but some passages were added as late as 1841—shortly before his death. And since not less than five of its drafts have been preserved, it is fairly easy to follow the various changes and mutations which brought it to the shape in which we know it.

This, incidentally, explains why *The Demon* is less compact in its structure than *The Novice*. It is also more romantic, at times even in an 'operatic' sense,[1] since the theme easily lends itself to such a treatment. Yet even when it becomes rhetorical, its rhetoric is of a high *poetic* order. There is a certain discrepancy between the gorgeous 'purple patches' in Lermontov's descriptions of the Caucasian scenery and the

---

[1] Anton Rubinstein turned it into an opera.

more reserved character of the narrative as such. But, then, the entire Caucasian *mise-en-scène* dates from the poet's last period, after the essentials of the narrative had already received their more or less final form.

Originally, *The Demon* must have been suggested to Lermontov by some foreign works, such as Byron's *Cain* and *Heaven and Earth*, Thomas Moore's *Love of the Angels*, and *Eloa* by Alfred de Vigny. The proud demon, or the 'sad spirit of exile' as he calls him, might even pass for a distant relative of Milton's Satan in *Paradise Lost*. In spite of that, the idea as well as the symbolic import of *The Demon* is undoubtedly Lermontov's own and can best be explained by further reference to one of his main dilemmas.

When Lermontov jotted down the first draft of this poem he also wrote a lyric called *My Demon*. He may have written it partly in imitation of a poem by Pushkin under the same title, but he expressed in it an attitude different from Pushkin's. Whereas Pushkin repudiated the spirit of negation, Lermontov frankly welcomed him as a 'sinister collection of evils'. Revelling in 'storms', his somewhat dandified demon keeps sowing diffidence wherever he appears. He despises love and prayer, and is as indifferent to bloodshed as he is to all lofty feelings.

Here we have obviously a romantic self-dramatization in the direction of evil. It is all very juvenile. But we must not forget that an essentially generous nature, if frustrated, often turns all its best impulses into their opposites, especially if these bear an aura of the romantic cult of evil. A Promethean impulse, if frustrated, can thus degenerate into its own 'demoniac' or 'satanic' contrast of the most destructive kind.[1] Lermontov, who had to put up with many a cruel frustration at an early age, enlarged (in 1831) the lyric in question by several 'satanic' traits, such as open scorn of kindness, love or pity. In another poem written in the same year he states quite definitely: 'Like my own Demon I am an elect of evil; like him I wander about proud and carefree—a stranger to heaven and earth.'

According to the Russian philosopher Vladímir Solovyëv, Lermontov's tragedy consisted in the gap between his genius and his low moral level. Instead of fighting the demoniac evil that was in him, he idealized it. But was this so? It may not be a mere coincidence that the earliest draft of *The Demon* was written almost at the same time as his poem *The Angel*. In both he expressed his uprootedness in terms of timeless realities. In *The Demon* he moreover gave a

[1] A Promethean romantic aims at the will to power, not in his own name and for his own sake, but for the sake of those 'suprahuman' values which transcend any purely personal ambitions. Nietzsche's Zarathustra is activated by such Promethean values. If he were deprived of his belief in them, he could easily fall a prey to utter cynicism and nihilism. In this case his 'will to power' might become purely personal and demoniacally destructive.

symbol of his ambivalent nature: not only his absorption in evil but also his sincere though ineffectual (and always frustrated) craving for what is good. This is why *The Demon*, in spite of any outside influences, can be regarded as one of Lermontov's most personal creations.

It is true that in a few lines preceding the first draft of the poem he says that the sad fancies embodied in it are only fruits of his 'inner emptiness'. Yet the next or second draft already contains a *Dedication* in which Lermontov is more explicit. For here he confesses not only to his cult of evil, but also to his craving for inner rebirth through love: 'Like my cold and cruel Demon, I enjoyed doing evil in this world; deceit was not new to me, and my heart was full of poison. But now, like that gloomy Genius, I have been reborn through your presence for innocent delights, for hope and freedom."

Evidently it was all a case of wishful thinking, since in a later *Dedication* the poet addresses his former sweetheart in entirely different terms. 'You will not recognize,' he says, 'the simple expression of the ennui (*toská*) which has tormented my poor mind for so many years, and the ravings of a sick soul will be regarded by you as nothing more than a fanciful dream.' It is significant that in the second draft of the poem the exiled Demon falls in love with a nun whose beauty is enough to make him crave for a return to his primeval state of bliss and goodness. But an angel is sent by God to protect her. The

Demon, being thus frustrated in his love, remains the same defiant spirit of evil and causes the nun to die in semi-madness. A similar *dénouement* can be found in the draft made in 1833—largely as a result of one of Lermontov's own unhappy loves.

The final version of *The Demon* was made by the poet during and after his stay in the Caucasus in 1837. In the previous drafts there was a rather vague Spanish setting. But in the fifth version (completed in 1838), with its magnificent Caucasian background, the blend of colour and verbal music is so powerful as to produce an unforgettable effect. Here Lermontov also modified the motif itself—most likely under the influence of an Ossetian folk-tale about the mountain demon infatuated with a beautiful mortal maiden. Having enlarged, or rather deepened, the symbolism of the poem, he gave it a metaphysical and at the same time a tragic personal meaning. This draft was later completed by a few minor additions and an Epilogue.[1]

4

Lermontov's Demon is, characteristically enough, a former angel who in the name of his own independence had rebelled against God. In punishment he was expelled from paradise and doomed

[1] Fragments of *The Demon* appeared in Krayévsky's periodical *Annals of the Fatherland* after the poet's death. The whole poem was first published abroad (at Karlsruhe) in 1856 and again in 1857.

to roam eternally throughout the universe. As a vindictive, sad exile he sowed evil wherever he appeared. But in the end evil itself began to bore him.

The only thing left to him was his proud though sterile isolation and his equally sterile freedom. But one day, when flying over the peaks of the Caucasus, the Demon saw amidst that scenery Tamara—a maiden of surpassing beauty, and fell in love with her. For the first time he thus loved a mortal woman and he was overwhelmed by this new experience. Determined not to yield her to anyone, he caused her betrothed and his escort to be killed on the eve of the wedding-day. In her bereavement Tamara entered a convent. But even here no peace was granted to her. Invisibly, the Demon descended into her cell night after night and whispered to her passionate words of love. As if regenerated by Tamara's beauty, the Demon felt that his love for her might reconcile him to life, to God and the Universe. 'I long for prayer and consolation; I long from now for faith in the good.' He was willing to forego his pride and rejoin the blissful throng of angels who had never tasted of sin, sadness or despair.

But while he tempts Tamara with words of love, her guardian angel confronts the Demon in order to protect her. The sight of his opponent only inflames the Demon to still greater passion. Leaving Tamara to her tempter, the angel—help-less and saddened—flies away. Tamara herself cannot but listen to the words of love; yet no sooner has the Demon touched her lips with the kiss of an immortal than she dies. Her soul is carried away by a messenger of God, while the Demon is doomed to dwell in the same void and loneliness till the end of time.

Evocative though it be in its imagery and music, *The Demon* is less compact than *The Novice*, partly because of the greater complexity of the theme itself. A few other shortcomings should be mentioned. In contrast to the Demon, who is energetic and persistent during his nocturnal visits, Tamara remains much too passive, almost mute. One also wonders at the passivity of the angel: obviously sent to protect her, he yet prefers to flee and leave Tamara to her fate. But these defects are trifling if compared with the wonderful passages abounding in the poem. Lermontov's description of the Kazbék group of mountains and of the Daryál Gorge (as seen by the flying Demon) is matchless in its colour, as well as in its mellow and caressing verbal harmonies. The poet's sure touch is equally marked in other scenes, above all in the more homely episode of Tamara surrounded by her girl-friends and dancing on the flat roof of her father's castle, while far away her bridegroom is being treacherously killed on his journey to the wedding. All said and done, *The Demon* is a masterpiece of Russian literature, but, like all great poetry, it is most difficult to translate.

Lermontov must have had certain misgivings about the too romantic character of *The Demon*; the more so because, while working at its final version, he was busy with such 'realistic' works as *A Treasurer's Wife*, *Sashka* and the terse Caucasian tale, *Begléts* (*The Fugitive*, 1839), describing the fate of a coward who left the battle-field and met with the kind of death he deserved. As if dissatisfied with the fantastic and meta-physical flavour of *The Demon*, he decided to write its ironical-realistic counterpart in the shape of a narrative poem under the title *A Tale for Children*.

Presumably started in 1840, this tale remained unfinished: it did not go beyond twenty-seven stanzas. While referring to *The Demon* as a mad childish delirium, Lermontov here promises to introduce us to an entirely different variety of the species. This time the Demon is nothing more than an ordinary fussy and vulgar Mephisto-pheles, or the kind of devil that appeared to Ivan Karamazov as a somewhat shabby, down-at-heel gentleman *qui frisait la cinquantaine*.

This terre-à-terre Mephistopheles falls in love with a St. Petersburg girl and at night, when everybody is asleep, he whispers to the dreaming girl the story of one of his former loves; all in a thoroughly realistic and ironic tone. In an old and half-derelict St. Petersburg palace (so he tells her) there lived Nina—a young beauty whose only companion was her aged and slightly crazy father. Whenever she entered the large empty hall of the palace, she was assailed by strange visions of love. At the age of seventeen she was taken to her first ball, where she made due impression upon society.

Here the fragment ends. It is impossible even distantly to conjecture as to what its continuation would have been like. All one can say is that the fragment itself is an excellent piece of work. Here, too, as in Pushkin's *Evgény Onégin*, conversational tone and diction are raised to the level of high poetry. Gogol regarded *A Tale for Children* as Lermontov's best tale in verse. He also saw in it (whether rightly or wrongly) an attempt at exorcising or sublimating the 'demoniac' element with which the poet was infected. 'It is possible that at the end of that tale he would have freed himself from the evil angel and at the same time from his melancholy (certain poems, such as *The Angel, A Prayer*, and a few others make one think so) had he only had more respect for his own talent.' [1]

Still, Lermontov was always dangerously fascinated by evil, in which he found more dynamic force than in its opposite. He realized only too well that this was the wrong kind of fascination, but there was something that interfered with his efforts to get rid of it. As if impelled to look the malady in the face, he decided at last to describe it with all the analytical power he could summon. This he did in his novel, *A Hero of our Time*.

[1] Gogol's *Passages from Correspondence with my Friends*.

V

The Hero and the Age

If the 1820's were the 'Golden Age' of Russian poetry, the following decade marked the gradual rise of Russian prose. The late eighteenth- and early nineteenth-century prose of Karamzín and his contemporaries sounded archaic at a time when France could boast of Balzac, England of Dickens and Thackeray, and Germany of the young Heine. So it was in the 1830's that Russian prose made the first strides which, some thirty years later, were to culminate in its great realistic novels—Russia's chief contribution to world literature. But even during that pioneering decade one could notice two main lines of prose-fiction, one represented by Pushkin and the other by Gogol.

Pushkin, with his flair for doing the right thing at the right time, started already in the later 1820's his unfinished novel, *Aráp Petrá Velíkogo* (*The Negro of Peter the Great*). This is a work of classical realism, depicting—in a parallel manner—the court of Versailles on the one hand, and that of the new Russian capital, St. Petersburg, on the other. The central hero of the novel was to be Pushkin's Abyssinian maternal great-grandfather Annibal, who had been bought by the Russian ambassador on the slave-market at Constantinople and sent as a present to Peter the Great. Yet in the six odd chapters preserved Peter himself is more conspicuous than any other character, although here, for once, he is shown in his more human and even homely moods.

In 1831 there appeared Pushkin's equally disciplined five stories under the common title *Póvesti Bélkina* (*Tales of Belkin*). They are not written but *told* stories—told by the 'late Iván Petróvich Bélkin', a genteel and pathetically comic narrator (of a fairly low social standing) whose inflection and manner of speaking are preserved throughout. This kind of story bears the Russian name of *skaz*,[1] and plays quite an important part in Russian fiction, Soviet fiction included.[2] Almost at the same time Pushkin was engaged in writing his novel *Dubróvsky*. Inspired by Sir Walter Scott, Pushkin yet wrote it in that terse prose of his own from which he would not desist even when taking up such a highly romantic or 'Hoffmannesque' theme as the one in his *Píkovaya Dáma* (*Queen of Spades*, 1836). And in his principal prosework, *A Captain's Daughter* (1836), the inspiration derived from Scott is combined with both Pushkin's simplicity and discipline at their best.

[1] From the verb *skazát'*, to tell.
[2] N. Leskóv and, after him, Alexéy Rémizov and Zamyátin became its acknowledged masters. In Soviet literature it was practised on a big scale by Zóshchenko.

Gogol's ornate and agitated prose has already been referred to. The 'furious' kind of prose imported from France found its chief representative in A. A. Bestúzhev-Marlínsky, whose romantic narratives (with frequent Caucasian settings) were immensely popular at the time. Among the more orthodox followers of Sir Walter Scott were M. N. Zagóskin, N. A. Polevóy and I. I. Lazhéchnikov, whereas Prince V. F. Odóyevsky and Alexander Véltman had been influenced by Jean Paul Richter and Sterne respectively.

Such were the salient features of Russian prose in the 1830's. Yet already at the beginning of the next decade there appeared two works which had a great influence upon the development of Russian fiction, especially after the acceptance of Belínsky's slogan of the 'natural school'. One of these two works was Lermontov's *A Hero of our Time* (1840), which adhered to the tradition of Pushkin. The other was Gogol's *Dead Souls* (1842), written in a prose different from, though complementary to, that of Pushkin. Here we are concerned with Lermontov's masterpiece.

2

Pechórin, the principal character of *A Hero of our Time*, is a descendant of Pushkin's Onégin, but with a difference. Lermontov's merit was that of all Russian authors he gave the first psychological portrait of such a 'superfluous' character and analysed him as a victim of the *Zeitgeist*, of the conditions he was doomed to live in. Hence the ironical label—a 'hero of our time'.

Pushkin's Onégin lived in the early 1820's, before the 'Decembrist' revolt. So he was able to pose and to relish his Byronic spleen to his heart's content. Pechórin, on the other hand, belonged to a later generation—the lost generation of the 1830's which had to pay the price for that abortive revolt. One of the principal consequences of the 'Decembrist' rising was the tightening of the police-regime and its clamping down on any individual will or initiative. Those who suffered most were the ambitious young men whose strength and talents found no outlet and were thus doomed to remain inactive. They were out of place in their own country. But if strength, especially great strength, is devoid of an adequate outlet, it invariably turns against itself and becomes destructive. Such was the tragedy of Pechórin.

And so in analysing him, Lermontov put his finger on the malady of an entire 'superfluous' generation, himself included. It is true that in his preface to the second edition of the novel he warns us not to confuse Pechórin's personality with that of the author. But such warnings are always somewhat suspect. Belínsky hit the nail on the head when declaring that Pechórin was a subjective projection of Lermontov without being actually autobiographic. It stands to reason that the author had projected into him a number of his own characteristics. In both of them frustrated strength was in danger of turning (and did turn) into a destructive, even a 'demoniacally' destructive, agency. Both were tired of love, of society, in fact of everything except the beauty of the Caucasian scenery. Both were equally prone to indulge in the same kind of callous egotism, since they could not believe in any true values outside or above their own immediate selves. Last but not least, Pechórin's encounter with Vera and her aged husband (in the section *Princess Mary*) is but another version of a similar meeting in *Princess Ligovskáya*, as well as in the play *The Two Brothers*—all of them referring to Lermontov's own painful encounter with the Bakhmétyevs in December 1835.

The novel was finished in 1839, but its first two editions appeared in 1840 and 1841 respectively. It is written in a prose which is less simple, perhaps, than the prose of Pushkin, yet it is even more flexible, while being equally disciplined and lucid. It has fewer gallicisms and is at the same time richly articulated because of its variety or even deliberate mixture of styles. The author's remarks and descriptions are alternated with the *skaz*-manner of Captain Maxím Maxímych—a kindly simple soul of the Bélkin variety. Then there are Pechórin's reminiscences and diaries, acute and coldly ironical like the man himself.

Pechórin's ordeals are unrolled before us not in their chronological order, but according to a definite psychological plan or pattern. The novel consists of five independent narratives joined together by the main character, and even more by the author who gives us all sorts of comments and necessary information. The narratives are constructed in a way reminiscent of Balzac's *La femme de trente ans* (1832) which Lermontov refers to in his novel.[1] The first two of the five narratives, *Bela* and *Maxím Maxímych*, show Pechórin as he is seen by others. Of the remaining three *Princess Mary* is in the form of Pechórin's diary, whereas *Tamán* and *The Fatalist* record some of his adventures—one in the Crimea and the other in the Caucasus. The central piece, *Princess Mary*, provides us above all with an analysis (or rather self-analysis) of Pechórin's mind and character.

3

The subject-matter of *Bela* is a distant echo of Pushkin's first Byronic tale in verse, *A Prisoner of the Caucasus*. The hero of that tale is a Russian officer captured by the Caucasian mountaineers. A primitive Caucasian belle falls in love with him; but he, being a civilized man, is much too blasé to respond to the girl's spontaneous feelings. He remains cool and callous even while she arranges all that is necessary for his escape, after which she commits suicide. In *Bela* we have a similar plot, in practically the same Caucasian

[1] Two other French works of importance he was undoubtedly familiar with were *Adolphe* by Benjamin Constant and *Confession d'un enfant du siècle* by de Musset.

setting. Only instead of being a captive, Pechórin is a society dandy sent—in punishment for a duel —to a remote fort held by the Russians. Here he serves as a junior officer under the command of Captain Maxím Maxímych. An honest old warrior with no social pretences, Maxím Maxímych is one of the finest figures in early Russian fiction. In a way he combines the characteristics of Pushkin's Mirónov (in *A Captain's Daughter*) and Bélkin. Yet, naive and kindly though he be, he is full of shrewd common sense, which cannot be said of his subaltern Pechórin.

In spite of the difference in character, education and social status, the Captain and Pechórin got on well together. Some estrangement arose between the two only after the bored dandy had taken a fancy to the Tartar girl Bela, the daughter of the local chieftain. Infatuated with Bela, Pechórin contrived to kidnap her with the help of her own brother whom he rewarded with a spirited horse —stolen from the girl's savage Tartar wooer Kazbích. Bela, frightened and diffident at first, soon fell in love with her captor. Even Maxím Maxímych became fond of her with a kind of disinterested fatherly affection. To quote his own words:

She was a very fine girl, Bela. In the end I got to feel towards her as if she had been my own daughter, and she became very fond of me. I should tell you that I have no near relatives to think about. For twenty years I have heard no news of my father or my mother. As for taking a wife, I never dreamed of doing so in my younger days, and it would be foolish to think of such a thing now. Naturally then I was glad to make a pet of Bela. She used to sing songs to us, or dance a Caucasian dance— the lezghinka. A wonderful dancer, she was. I have watched our fine young ladies in their ballroom dances at the provincial capital, and twenty years ago I was at a swagger ball in Moscow; but that sort of dancing was not in the same street with Bela's for beauty. Gregóry Alexándrovich (Pechórin) decked her out like a doll, pampered and fondled her, and it was a marvel the way in which her beauty increased. The tan disappeared from her face and hands, so that in the end her cheeks were quite rosy. She was always cheerful and I never wanted anything in the world except to make her laugh, God rest her soul.[1]

The last exclamation points to Bela's tragic end—inevitable when in love with such a man as Pechórin. For no sooner had he noticed that Bela truly loved him than he lost all interest in her. It was not love he had been after, but conquest and the egoistic feeling of his own power over her. One day, when Pechórin was out on a hunting expedition, Bela left her room and went for a little walk outside the walls. Here she

[1] All the passages are taken from *A Hero of our Time*, translated by Eden and Cedar Paul (Allen & Unwin).

was mortally wounded by Kazbích, who had been prowling about the fort. Bela's agony ends this part of the novel.

It is Captain Maxímych who tells the author the story, while travelling in his company along the Georgian military road in the heart of the Caucasus. His own style—the style of a *skaz*—is now and then interrupted by the author's remarks or descriptions of the scenery, and the alternation of the two styles adds to the interest and the atmosphere of the narrative.

Maxím Maxímych, the second story of the novel, tells us in a sober, matter-of-fact language how the author had lodged at an inn in Vladikavkáz where, one day later, he was joined by Maxím Maxímych. Suddenly they heard that Pechórin had stopped there, on his way to Persia. Maxím Maxímych was overjoyed at the prospect of meeting, after such a lapse of time, his old friend and fellow-officer, linked with him through the tragedy of Bela. Impatient to see Pechórin, he sent word to him that his old captain was at the inn. Maxím Maxímych was sure that the young man would come rushing to embrace him. But the blasé society dandy was in no hurry to see his former friend and superior. When at last he came, he was cold and politely aloof: an aristocratic snob condescendingly talking to an effusive, warm-hearted commoner. The Captain's consternation was so great that he could not get over it. Fortunately, Pechórin and his arrogant flunkey departed without delay.

We had long ceased to hear the bells of the troika, or the grind of the wheels on the flinty road (says the author), but my poor old friend continued to stand where he was, deep in thought.

'Yes,' he said at last, with assumed indifference, though tears of vexation were brimming over from his eyes and coursing down his cheeks, 'of course we were close friends long ago. But what does he care about me now I am neither rich nor a high official, and I am much older than he is. Did you notice what a dandified rig-out he was wearing? He might still have been at St. Petersburg. A smart calash, too. Such a lot of luggage, and a footman with damnable side.'

Such was the encounter of the two former friends—one of them a man of the people, and the other a self-absorbed man of society. Yet this was not the whole of Pechórin. Something deeper had awakened in him during Bela's agony and death, though not for long: whatever his feelings, the mask of indifference was regarded by him as something obligatory. Like many an isolated and rootless individual he refused to, or else could not, draw a line between the mask and the man, the sham and the substance.

Of the next three narratives, *Tamán* is a superbly told story [1] in which Lermontov recalls

[1] Chekhov regarded it as the best story in Russian literature.

(in Pechórin's words) his own adventure—among 'honest smugglers'—in the port of that name during his first exile to the Caucasus. Then follows *Princess Mary* the whole of which is a fine piece of psychological dissection in the form of a diary. The novel ends with that concentrated tale, *The Fatalist*, describing a strange incident Lermontov himself might have witnessed in a Caucasian Cossack settlement. The longest of these three narratives, *Princess Mary*, is also the central piece of the novel. As such it calls for special comment.

4

The happenings told in this story take place in the fashionable Caucasian spa of Pyatigórsk, and some of them may relate to Lermontov and his acquaintances. Várya Lopúkhina emerges here as Vera, and her husband as the gouty Prince Ligovskóy. The pseudo-romantic poseur Grushnítsky is usually identified with Major Martýnov, whose bullet was later to kill the poet.[1] The caustic doctor Werner again portrays a certain Doctor Meyer whom he had met at Stavrópol and whom he liked. Lermontov's description of the fashionable set at Pyatigórsk in the 1830's sounds authentic, although here too he was evidently not regarded as respectable enough to be accepted by the 'cream of society'.

[1] Another surmise is that Grushnítsky was a portrait of a certain P. L. Kolyubákin, notorious as a quarrelsome person and a duellist.

The story, simple in its plot, is complicated psychologically. Pechórin, while staying in the spa, starts from sheer boredom a love-intrigue with Princess Mary—an inexperienced young beauty courted by the shallow poseur Grushnítsky. But once Pechórin has become sure of the girl's love he begins to cool off and loses all interest in her. New complications arise when Vera (his old love) and her husband enter the scene. Vera's jealousy, Pechórin's chivalrous defence of Princess Mary and Grushnítsky's envy bring matters to a climax at the moment when Pechórin has renewed his love with Vera, leaving the trusting Princess Mary to her own despair. A duel follows in which Grushnítsky is killed. When Pechórin returns from the duel he finds to his chagrin that Vera and her husband have left the spa. He has a last conversation with Princess Mary to whom he callously declares that he had not meant anything serious when trying to win her affections. In consequence of his duel with Grushnítsky, he is sent to the very fortress in which his life was to become so strangely intertwined with Bela's and the old-world Captain Maxím Maxímych's.

'And now,' he wrote in his diary, 'here in this wearisome fort, I often review the past, and ask myself why I was unwilling to tread on the road opened to me by fate, a road where gentle pleasures and peace of mind awaited me. But no, I could never have become reconciled to it. I am like a seaman who was born and bred on the deck of a pirate ship. He has become so accustomed to storms and battles that on land he feels insufferably bored, however alluring the shady woods, however temperate the sunshine.'

The quoted passage is typical of a *déraciné* such as Pechórin who, being in love with his own pain, does not mind inflicting pain upon others. In this respect he bears, for all his concreteness, traces of a romantic-demoniac character at a time when such a 'hero' was already getting out of fashion and had begun to look more comical than sinister even in romantic fiction. Yet Lermontov succeeded: partly because he himself gave—in Grushnítsky—a magnificent parody of such a type, and partly because Pechórin's actions are stated with psychological convincingness. He is shown, moreover, as an intensified egotist of the 1830's who, finding nothing that is worth while outside himself, cannot but extol and gratify his own ego.

I see the sufferings and the joys of others only in relation to myself, I regard them as food to nourish my spiritual strength. It has become impossible for me to do foolish deeds under the stimulus of passion. In me ambition has been crushed by circumstances to assume another form. For ambition is nothing other than the thirst for power, and my chief delight is to impose my will upon all with whom I come in contact. To inspire in others feelings of love, devotion, or fear, what is it but the first sign and the greatest triumph of power. To be for someone a cause of suffering or joy, without the least right—can pride know sweeter food than this? What indeed is happiness? Gratified pride?

All this cannot be accepted as an excuse for Pechórin's behaviour towards Bela and Princess Mary, but it offers at least an explanation. His stress on the 'will to power', combined with his unscrupulous 'beyond good and evil' where other people are concerned, contains all the germs of nihilism. But there is also a tragic side to it.

The critic and poet Apollón Grigóryev (he was active in the early 1860's) defined Pechórin as 'weakness of stilted self-will'. A closer definition would be: real strength gone wrong; the strength of a man endowed with talents, will and ambition, but all to no purpose. Being unable to believe in such a thing as a purpose, Pechórin is doomed to be either a mere analytical observer, or else an experimenter exercising his own futile 'will to power' without any use either to himself or to others, and spelling disaster to everyone he meets. He knows that in essence he is a 'cripple', yet he cannot help it.

As a tragic *déraciné* of the 1830's Pechórin is the most important link between Pushkin's Onégin and the 'superfluous men' in subsequent Russian fiction. At the same time he is merciless in his self-analysis, although without any moralizing propensity. As Lermontov explains in his preface to the second edition of the novel: 'Let me beg you, however, not to jump to the conclusion that the author of this book aspires to become a reformer of public morals. God forbid! I found it agreeable to sketch a contemporary as he presented himself to me—and, unfortunately both for him and for you, I have met him too often. The illness has been diagnosed, but goodness alone knows how to cure it.'

5

Lermontov is supposed to have intended to write a trilogy of novels—one about the epoch of Catherine II, another about that of Alexander I and one dealing with the period of Nicholas I. If so, then *A Hero of our Time* would represent the last part of such a planned trilogy—a part for which the material was ready at hand.

What matters, though, is the fact that in producing *A Hero of our Time* he presented Russian literature with one of its great novels—a novel in which all the characters (with the possible exception of Vera) are drawn with consummate art. Less known, and even less appreciated abroad than many other masterpieces of Russian prose, this work is yet a classic. Belínsky, who had sponsored it at once, remained one of its enthusiastic admirers in the very teeth of its detractors. Gogol himself said, in his *Passages from Correspondence with Friends*, that 'no one in our country has written so far such magnificent and full-blooded prose. Here he (Lermontov) evidently penetrated deeper into the realities of existence; he promised to become a great painter of Russian life, but sudden death has deprived us of him.'

A Hero of our Time has even been admired by some critics as the greatest Russian novel. It certainly is the first truly psychological novel in Russian literature. As far as an insight into certain aspects of the psychology of nihilism is concerned, Lermontov anticipated Dostoévsky. After all, from Pechórin to Stavrógin (the hero of *The Possessed*) there is only one step; and not a big one at that. Lermontov's natural and flexible prose, on the other hand, was not without influence on the prose of both Turgénev and Tolstóy. One ought to stress, perhaps, also the cathartic nature of this novel, since Lermontov projected into Pechórin some of those features he himself wanted to get rid of. Such a conclusion is borne out by several poems he wrote at the time. And this brings us to a survey of Lermontov's poetry written during the last four years of his life.

VI

The Last Phase

I

By the time Lermontov had reached the summit
of his creative power, the high standard of taste
and craftsmanship, associated with the 'Golden
Age' of Russian poetry in the 1820's, was already
on the decline. And so was the general interest in
poetry as such. Where poetic technique was still
paramount—in the works of Baratýnsky and
Tyútchev, for instance—it was less appreciated
than before. Even Lermontov's first flash of
fame at the beginning of 1837 had been caused
by the civic rather than the aesthetic side of his
invective. The success—such as it was—of his
collected poems in 1840 was due mainly to the
enthusiasm with which Belínsky welcomed it.
The volume (which contained also the final
version of *The Novice*) was fairly slender, but its
quality was high indeed, since Lermontov had
wisely eliminated everything his artistic conscience did not approve of. Thus of all his
youthful poems *The Angel* alone was included—
the rest was ignored. It should be noted, though,
that in addition to that volume, Lermontov completed his poetic work by writing in 1840 and

1841 some of his finest verse.[1] The poetry of his last phase can, on the whole, be divided, for convenience sake, into four groups: personal meditative lyrics, poems of indictment, poems with a folkloristic flavour, and a few truly excellent descriptive poems. All told, it was during the last two years that Lermontov achieved the kind of poetic perfection which entitled him to a place second only to Pushkin.

It has already been mentioned that, as time went on, Lermontov kept returning to the same themes and motifs. He did this either in order to give them a more perfect shape (as in *The Novice* and *The Demon*), or to take certain passages from an older poem and include them, for better effect, in a new creation: like an artist making use of his old sketches for mature works of art. Thus his *Póle Borodiná* (*The Field of Borodinó*, 1830–31) was recast by him, six years later, into one of his best poems—*Borodinó*. He even took up some of Pushkin's themes not in order to imitate them, but to change or modify them in his own way. He did this with the prophet-theme, for instance. In Pushkin's famous poem *Prorók* (*The Prophet*) the seer is summoned by God Himself to 'burn with His word the hearts of men'. In Lermontov's poem under the same title we find, however, the reverse of such a finale. His prophet is

---

[1] Many of those poems were written in the Caucasus. The year 1837, too, the year of his Caucasian exile, was rather prolific in this respect, the crop of his short poems being much smaller in 1836, 1838 and 1839.

regarded by the crowd not as a messenger of God, but as an impostor and an outcast, since he is so different from the respectable human average. He is jeered at by all and sundry, and children are duly warned by their parents never to follow his example.

Lermontov's lyric *Vétka Palestíny* (*A Twig from Palestine*) was obviously inspired by Pushkin's poem *Tsvetók* (*The Flower*), but Lermontov worked out the motif in his own independent manner. The same can be said of *Kinzhál* (*The Dagger*)—a theme tackled by both. Another example is Pushkin's *Razgovór Knigoprodávtsa s Poétom* (*A Dialogue between the Bookseller and the Poet*), in which the poet's *profession de foi* is expressed in verse sparkling with wit, commonsense and humour. He sees the facts of life as they are, and makes the best of them without rancour or indignation. Lermontov's analogous poem *Zhurnalíst, chitátel i pisátel* (*The Journalist, the Reader and the Writer*), is filled however with a good deal of irony, spite and invective. *Tri Pálmy* (*Three Palms*) is another poem the motif of which Lermontov took from Pushkin in order to work it out in a pessimistic spirit—so different from Pushkin's treatment.

Nor is it without interest to consider the few translations Lermontov made during those last few years of his life. Schiller, for example, was now forgotten. Byron, on the other hand, still remained the poet's favourite, and he translated (in 1836) one of Byron's *Hebrew Melodies*, as well

as *Lines Written in an Album at Malta*. From
Heine he paraphrased (in 1841) *Ein Fichtenbaum
steht einsam* (*A firtree stands lonely*) and *Sie liebten
sich beide* (*They both loved each other*). Even one of
Lermontov's finest lyrics, *Utës* (*The Crag*, 1841),
must have been inspired by Heine. His para-
phrases of Goethe's *Des Wanderer's Nachtlied*
(*The Wanderer's Night-song*) and Zedlitz's *Das
Geisterschiff* (*The Ghostship*) were made a year
earlier. Incidentally, the paraphrase of Zedlitz's
poem and *Poslédnee novosélye* (*The Last Housewarming*, 1841) were Lermontov's homage to
Napoleon—a cult which he shared with Heine.

2

Whatever Lermontov wrote during this period
bears the stamp of a fully mature poet. Economy,
precision, melodiousness, a kind of Pushkinian
naturalness and ease—such are the principal
virtues of his verse. In addition, his poems of
indictment show an intensity which ranges from
the lashing invectives of his *Meditation* to the
bitterness of his *Blagodárnost* (*Gratitude*, 1840),
addressed to God and vibrating with the wrath-
ful irony of a defeated metaphysical rebel:

> For all, for all my thanks to Thee I offer,
> For passion's martyrdom that no one knew,
> For poisoned kisses, for the grief I suffer,
> Vengeance of foes, slander of friends untrue,
> For the soul's ardour squandered in waste
>   places,

For everything in life that cheated me—
But see that now and after such Thy grace is
That I no longer must give thanks to Thee.[1]

Even his wonderful *Borodinó* (1837) is an indictment by implication. Outwardly the poem consists of a Russian veteran's account of how the French army of invasion received its first blow on the plain of Borodinó. The account is done in the quiet folk-style, yet the veteran's story is interrupted now and then by the refrain which is hardly flattering to the descendants of those warriors:

> Yes, in our time were men,
> And from the field of battle then
> How few returned,
> How few returned the fields to till!
> Heroes—not lads like you—they still
> Fought on . . .[2]

A different indictment is *The Last Housewarming* written in 1841, when, amidst great solemnities, Napoleon's ashes were brought from St. Helena to Paris and buried in the *Palais des Invalides*. The poet sums up the irresponsible callousness with which the French had deserted Napoleon in the hour of crisis, and the equally irresponsible enthusiasm with which they now welcomed his mortal remains. 'A miserable and shallow people'—such is his verdict.

[1] Translated by C. M. Bowra in *A Book of Russian Verse* (Macmillan).

[2] Translated by Frances Cornford and Esther Polyanóvsky Salaman in *Poems from the Russian* (Faber).

Poems of this kind, intense though they be, express, however, only one aspect of Lermontov's Muse. He needed them as an outlet for his indignation and disgust in a society and a system with which he had nothing in common. Still, no one can thrive on disgust alone, or on isolation. And Lermontov was no exception. Like his own Demon, he knew that even behind his 'cult of evil' there smouldered a desire for reconciliation with life. As reconciliation through a great and powerful love had been frustrated in him, he was on the look-out for other possibilities. There were even moments when his longing assumed religious or semi-religious aspects. Two of his best-known poems of that period (one written in 1837 and the other two years later) actually bear the title *Molítva* (*A Prayer*). A kind of quasi-mystical flash is perceptible also at the end of his fine nature poem, beginning with the line, 'When o'er the yellowing corn a fleeting shadow rushes' (1837). His contact with the beauties of Nature makes him forget the worries of life, however brief such moments:

> Then does my troubled soul find solace for a
>   while,
> Then vanish for a time the furrows from my
>   brow,
> And happiness is mine a moment here below,
> And in the skies I see God smile.[1]

[1] Translated by Walter Morison in *A Book of Russian Verse*, ed. by C. M. Bowra.

Communion with Nature was bound to awaken Lermontov's interest in those peasant masses who (in contrast with society) stood close to Nature, or still were part and parcel of her. A proof of his sympathetic interest in them is his poem *Borodinó*, or his portrait of Maxím Maxímych—a man close to the people—in *A Hero of our Time*. Lermontov was moreover keenly alive also to the beauties of Russian folk-poetry, and his grasp of the folk-spirit came out in his amazing *Pésnya pro tsaryá Ivána Vasílyevicha, molodógo opríchnika i udalógo kuptsá Kaláshnikova* (*A Song about Tsar Ivan Vasilyevich, his Young Body-Guard, and the Valiant Merchant Kalashnikov*, 1837). This perfect creation is so steeped in the *bylíny* and the historical folk-songs of the Russian people that Belínsky rated it even higher than Pushkin's delightful poetic transposition of folklore in his *Skázki* (*Fairy Tales*).

Even before Pushkin, folkloristic themes and motifs had been taken up by Vasily Zhukóvsky. But Zhukóvsky treated them in the 'German' fashion: while making use of folk-motifs he left out their peculiar verbal style and pattern. Lermontov, on the other hand, knew how to assimilate both. The theme for this lay about Ivan the Terrible, the favourite hero of historical Russian folk-songs, was probably suggested to him by Kirsha Danílov's *Drévniye rossíyskie stikhotvoréniya* (*Ancient Russian Poems*), a belated Russian counterpart of Percy's *Reliques*. It contains seventy *bylíny*, collected in 1781 but published in

1804 and again in 1818. Nor was Lermontov ignorant of the work done in this particular field by the enthusiastic collector Peter Kiréyevsky. Yet whatever the sources and influences, he preserved the genuine style and spirit of the people not only in the language but also in the figures of his lay. His 'awe-inspiring' Tsar might have sprung from the people's imagination. The same can be said of the 'valiant merchant' Kaláshnikov who prefers to face the executioner's axe rather than cast a slur upon his wife. The arrogant bodyguard who had molested her was slain by the merchant in a public fist fight. Asked by the Tsar whether he had killed his opponent deliberately or by mere chance, he answered that he had killed him deliberately, knowing full well that such an answer would cost him his own life.

In this rhapsody Lermontov made skilful use of the rhythmic devices so abundant in the *byliny*, and also of the dactylic endings—a practice applied to some of his lyrics as well. A further proof of Lermontov's contact with folk-poetry and folklore is his widely popular *Kazáchya kolybélnaya pésnya* (*A Cossack Cradle Song*). Presumably suggested to him by Scott's *Lullaby of an Infant Chief*, it yet has the authentic accent of a Cossack mother rocking her baby to sleep. While in the Caucasus, Lermontov took a keen interest not only in the native tribes, but also in the Russian Cossack settlements scattered all over the place. Traces of the Caucasian Cossack folklore can be found in the poem, *Darý Teréka*

(*The Gifts of the Terek*) and in the motif of his *Son* (*Dream*) beginning with the line, 'In midday heat in the vale of Dagestan'. A closer personal contact with those Cossacks, as well as with the soldier masses in general, was made however by Lermontov during the battles and skirmishes with the rebellious mountaineers. Nothing binds people more closely together than common dangers—an experience recorded by him in one of his finest poems describing the battle on the Caucasian river Valerík (near Grózny).

3

The directness and simplicity, typical of Lermontov's last period, come out best of all in his description of this battle in which he himself took part on 11 July 1840. The poem is often called simply *Valerík*. It begins like an informal letter to a woman-friend. Lermontov may have had in mind Várya Lopúkhina, who still kept haunting his memory. Gradually however this longish rhymed letter passes into a description of battle scenes, but not in the rhetorical 'grand' manner. It is mainly trifles and obvious incidents of a battle that follow one another, yet they are rendered with such vivid and convincing poetic realism as to be unforgettable because of their very simplicity. No wonder an echo of this poem is felt in Tolstóy's Caucasian story, *Nabég* (*A Raid*), and even in the battle-scenes of his *War and Peace*.

Lermontov's poetic realism reached a climax also in his *Zaveshchánie (Testament)*. This poem was written at the same time as *Valerík*, but it describes only one poignant episode: the last wishes of a dying soldier. The whole of it is a monologue of a mortally wounded officer who addresses his friend and comrade-in-arms due to leave for their far-off native district. The four-footed iambics of the poem retain throughout an ordinary conversational inflection, and the two interwoven motifs of love and death are all the stronger because of their understatement. The artistic effect of the poem is not lost even in a translation.

I want to be alone with you,
A moment quite alone,
The minutes left to me are few,
They say I'll soon be gone,
And you are going home on leave,
They say . . . but why, I don't believe
There is a soul who'll greatly care
To hear about me over there.

And yet if someone questions you,
Whoever it may be—
Tell them a bullet hit me through
The chest,—and did for me.
And say I died there for the Tsar,
And say what fools our doctors are—
And that I took you by the hand
And spoke about my native land.

My father and my mother both
By now are surely dead.
To tell the truth I would be loth
To cause them tears to shed.
If one of them is living, say
I'm bad at writing home, and they
Have told the regiment to pack—
And that I shan't be coming back.

We had a neighbour as you know,
And you remember I
And she . . . How very long ago
It is we said goodbye.
She won't ask after me, nor care;
But tell her ev'rything, don't spare
Her empty heart; and let her cry:—
To her it doesn't signify.[1]

It was during those years that Lermontov tried
to establish also a more intimate personal contact
with the very soil of true Russia—the Russia of
the people. This longing found a vigorous expression in his poem *Ródina* (*My Country*, 1841).
What is dear to him in his native land is neither
'glory bought with blood' nor proud historical
traditions, but the vast Russian landscape with
its brooding steppes, floods and forests, its
stubble fields, lanes, cottages and the *moujiks*
whom he is ready to accept (like Alexander Blok
some seventy years after him) with all their
rowdiness.

[1] Translated by Maurice Baring.

And many a feast-day evening I am found
Eager to watch upon the dewy ground
Till dawn is near,
The tramp and whistle of the dance and hear
The drunken babble round.[1]

4

Such moods and endeavours, however genuine,
were no longer enough to save Lermontov from
himself. In essentials, at any rate, he was too
much estranged from life and from human beings
to come to terms with either. Pechórin's nihilism
persisted in him, and there was no remedy to
exorcise it. Haunted by the boredom of an
isolated *enfant du siècle* as well as by the 'dread of
the days to come', he found the whole of existence increasingly tedious and meaningless.

Oh gloomy and dreary! And no one to stretch
    out a hand
In the years when the soul nears disaster. . . .
Desire! But what use is an empty desire with-
    out end?
And the years, the best years but fly faster.[2]

Is it then surprising that the death-wish, having
been latent in Lermontov for years, flared up
again and again in the poetry of his last period,
beginning with the ironical *Gratitude*? Even his

[1] Quoted from *Poems from the Russian*, translated by
Frances Cornford and Esther Polyanóvsky Salaman
(Faber).

[2] Translated by C. M. Bowra, *op. cit.*

communion with Nature could no longer stave it off. He now tried to find in the phenomena of Nature herself symbolic analogies with his own fate. His poignantly beautiful lyric, *The Crag*, is but another expression of his own hopeless loneliness. In one of his poems he compares himself to a withered leaf torn from its branch and tossed about in the gale—a simile often used in romantic poetry, from Arnault's *La Feuille* (1816) onwards. Even in Goethe's *A Wanderer's Nightsong* Lermontov paraphrased the line, *Warte nur, balde ruhest du auch* (*Wait only, thou too shalt rest*), in such a way as to give it the meaning of eternal rest. In one of his last poems, beginning with the line, *Vykhozhú odín ya na dorógu* (Lone I walk onto the pathway), he is overawed by the beauty of the night when the 'plain listens to God and star communes with star'. Yet all he can wish for amidst that silent splendour is oblivion and eternal sleep.

Despair, having for a long time alternated in him with anger and protest, finally took the upper hand, the death-wish in its wake. He became obsessed with the actual premonition of death—prowling and waiting round the corner. Thus in the early months of 1841, while planning to leave the army and give all his time to literature, he yet could not get rid of the idea that he was soon to die. There are at least three reliable witnesses to whom he spoke about it: Count Sollogúb, the poetess Countess Evdókia Rostópchina and the young Slavophil Yúry Samárin.

What followed on 27 July in the environs of Pyatigórsk was only an endorsement of his own premonition. Was his duel with Major Martýnov a suicide by proxy? It looks more than probable that Lermontov died because he wanted to die.

VII

Conclusion

It is idle to speculate what Lermontov might or might not have achieved had he not died at an age when many great talents only begin to develop. The measure of his creative power is the fact that, in spite of his untimely death, he had yet secured for himself one of the foremost places in Russian literature. It is true that, in contrast to Pushkin's harmonious and classically balanced genius, Lermontov represents the restless, questing and rebellious element in the Russian consciousness. Yet the aesthetic value of his work at its best is so great that his mature creations belong to the cultural equipment of every educated Russian.

The various facets of Lermontov's work have influenced a number of Russian poets and writers, Turgénev, Tolstóy and Dostoévsky included. The 'civic' aspect of his poetry, with its passionate indictments, was taken up and continued above all by Nikolái A. Nekrásov (1824–78). Its introspective and meditative side affected Herzen's friend and fellow-exile in London—the poet Nikolái Ogarëv (1819–98), as well as that sensitive though somewhat belated romantic Yákov Polónsky (1819–98). In the present century he found an admirer in the leading Russian symbolist Alexander Blok (1880–1921), and another in the 'poet's poet' of Soviet literature, Borís Pasternák (*b.* 1890).

As to his popularity abroad, Lermontov owes it in the first place to his novel, *A Hero of our Time*. Translated into all European languages, it is now regarded as one of the world classics. In addition, Lermontov's enigmatic personality, or rather its impact upon his genius, will continue to puzzle those lovers of literature who are interested in the deeper and more complex processes of a creative mind. One can safely say that the intrinsic value of Lermontov's work as a whole has not diminished with the passage of time. On the contrary, it has proved to be great enough to make each successive generation find some further aspects of its significance.

BIOGRAPHICAL NOTE

1814   Born in Moscow on 15 October (new style).

1817   Death of his mother.

1827–30 Studied at the 'Pension noble' in Moscow.

1830–32 Moscow University.

1832–34 The School of Cavalry Cadets, St. Petersburg.

1834   Ensign in the Hussar Regiment at Tsárskoe Seló.

1835   *Hadji Abrék* published.

1835–36 *The Boyar Orsha.*

1837   *The Death of a Poet.* Exiled to the Caucasus.

        A Song about Tsar Iván Vasílyevich, his Young Body-Guard and the Valiant Merchant Kaláshnikov.

1838   Reinstated in his Hussar Regiment. *A Treasurer's Wife* published.

1839   *The Fugitive*; *The Novice* (finished); *Sáshka.*

1840   Duel with de Barante. Second exile to the Caucasus. His collected poems, *Stikhotvoréniya*, published. First edition of *A Hero of our Time.*

1841   Second edition of *A Hero of our Time.* He was shot dead in a duel with Major Martýnov on 27 July (new style).

1856   *The Demon* first published (at Karlsruhe).

BIBLIOGRAPHY

The best Russian editions of Lermontov's works: The Academy edition 1910; *Pólnoe sobránie sochinéniy* (4 vols.), edited by B. M. Eichenbaum, 1939, 1947; the SSSR Academy edition (6 vols.) 1954–57; *Sobránie sochinéniy* (4 vols.), edited by J. L. Andrónikov, D. D. Blagóy, and Yu. G. Oksman, 1957.

ENGLISH TRANSLATIONS

Translations of *The Demon*: by A. C. Stephens 1875; E. Storr 1894; Ellen Richter 1910; Robert Burness 1918; Gerald Shelley, 1930.

The Circassian Boy (*The Novice*), translated by S. S. Conant, Boston, 1875.

The Song about the Merchant Kalashuikov, translated by E. L. Voynich, 1911; by John Cowinos, 1929.

Translations of *A Hero of our Time*. An anonymous version under the title *Sketches of Russian Life in the Caucasus* appeared in 1853. Two translations, one by David Bogue and the other by Therese Pulszky, were published in 1854. Further translations were made: by J. M. Wisdom and M. Murrey, 1912; by John Swinnerton Phillimore, 1920; by Reginald Merton, 1928; by Eden and Cedar Paul, 1940 (Second Edn. 1958).

Various poems by Lermontov in English translations: *A Book of Russian Verse*, 1943, and

A Second Book of Russian Verse, 1947, ed. by C. M. Bowra; *Poems from the Russian* by Frances Cornford and Esther Polyanóvsky Salaman, 1925; *Russian Poetry* by Babette and Avrahm Yarmolinsky, 1930; *Pushkin, Lermontov, Tyutchev, Poems*, translated by V. Nabokov, 1947; *A Treasury of Russian Verse*, ed. by A. Yarmolinsky, 1949. For some further particulars consult *Lermontov in English*, by Anna Heifetz, 1942.

FRENCH TRANSLATIONS

Le Démon, translated by P. Pélan al'Angers, 1858; T. Anossov, 1860; S. de Biram, 1884; M. de C. (Geneva), 1888; Benjamin Detraut, 1892; Princesse E. Orbeliani, 1907.

Un héros du siècle, translated by M. Stolypine, 1843; without the translator's name in *L'Illustration*, 1846; *Un Héros de notre temps*, translated by J. M. Chopin, 1853; Edouard Sheffter, 1855; A. de Villamarie, 1886 and 1905.

Chefs d'oeuvres poétiques de Lermontoff, translated by P. Péladan d'Angers, 1866.

Oeuvres de Lermontoff, translated by L. Briavoine de Lahey (St. Petersburg), 1876.

Les perles de la poésie slave par Henrí Grégoire (Liège), 1918.

Les cent chefs d'oeuvres étrangers (XIII) par Louis Jousserandot, 1919.

GERMAN TRANSLATIONS

Der Dæmon, translated by T. Opitz, 1859; L. von Osten, 1878.

Der Novize, translated by Roman Baron von Budberg—Beninghausen, 1842.

Poetischer Nachlass Michail Lermontoffs, translated by Friedrich Bodenstert, 1852.

Bela, translated by Varnhagen von Ense, 1840.

Der Held unserer Zeit, translated by Dr. August Bolty, 1852; by W. Lange, 1877.

Lermontoffs Werke, Herausgegeben von Arthur Luther (in Meyers Klassiker Ausgaben), 1922.

SOME BIOGRAPHICAL AND CRITICAL STUDIES

In Russian: by V. I. Pokróvsky, 1905; D. S. Merezhkóvsky, 1909, 1911; N. A. Kotlyarévsky, 1912; D. N. Ovsyániko-Kulikóvsky, 1914; S. V. Shuválov, 1925; L. Ya. Ginsburg, 1940; N. L. Brodsky, 1945; I. L. Andrónikov, 1951; S. V. Ivánov, 1952; A. N. Sokolóv, 1952.

Zhizn i tvórchestvo M. Yu. Lérmontova, 1941.

Literatúrnæ Naslédstvo 43/44, 45/46, 1941.

Lérmontov v rússkoy krítike, ed. by Zénov, 1951.

In other languages:

E. Duchesne, *Michel Lermontov*, 1910.

H. Troyat, *L'étrange destinée de Lermontov*, 1952.

F. Duckmayer, *Die Einführung Lermontovs in Deutschland und des Dichters Persönlichkeit*, 1925.